Dimensional® Selling™

Building Productive Relationships

V.R. Buzzotta, Ph.D. • R.E. Lefton, Ph.D.

A NOTE ABOUT GENDER-SPECIFIC LANGUAGE: Anyone who has written anything longer than a grocery list knows that the English language provides a finite number of methods to eliminate gender from one's writing. We have made every effort to exclude partiality from this book. Our intent was to present a balanced work that demonstrates our high regard for both women and men in management.

For written permission:

Psychological Associates
8201 Maryland Avenue
St. Louis, MO 63105 U.S.A.

International Standard Book Number 0-9630421-5-7

Printed in the United States of America

Table of Contents

Acknowledgements

From the time the initial concept was expressed years ago, through the completion of this manuscript, *Dimensional Selling* has had many contributors. For all the support and encouragement along the way, the authors wish to thank the following people:

We owe a debt of gratitude to the staff of Psychological Associates, who have helped refine these ideas through the years, particularly to Mannie Sherberg, who helped write the earliest editions of this book, and to Larry Gross, who worked so diligently to make this most recent edition more direct and reader-friendly. We gratefully acknowledge the contribution of Roger Heape, Ph.D., whose support in research, content revision, and editing was invaluable; and Dorothy Saeger for her careful editing of the manuscript. We also wish to thank Bob Buzzotta and Paula Hawkins for their contributions to the graphic appearance of the book and its dust jacket.

Of course, if we were to acknowledge all who have contributed to the common sense principles expressed in this book, we would have to include the many psychologists and behavioral scientists who have codified and tested our common sense knowledge of why people and groups behave as they do; we would also have to list the many insightful classical Asian, Greek, Roman, and European writers who have described so clearly the basic reasons humans behave as they do.

Perhaps the most telling proof that these principles work is offered by your own experience both in and out of the work place. We hope you will evaluate this book's content through that very personal prism.

Vic Buzzotta
Bob Lefton
St. Louis, Missouri, USA
August 2000

CHAPTER 1

Selling, People Skills, and You

If you think of selling as a form of persuading, you realize it's something we all do. Although salespeople and sales managers are paid to do it, just about everyone who works for a living must occasionally sell to (or persuade) others.

For example, Helen Wright manages the accounting department at a trucking company. You won't find "selling" in her job description. Today, however, she wants to talk to her company's data-processing manager to persuade him to process cash-flow reports semiweekly instead of weekly. Because the manager thinks his department is already overloaded, he won't be enthusiastic. Helen has some selling to do.

Or consider Lou Parrish. He's the shipping foreman for a major shoe manufacturer. Sales work is not usually part of his regular duties, either. However, today he will try to persuade one of his packers to change the way he packs shoe boxes into cartons so more boxes will fit into each carton. The packer is a hothead who doesn't take advice well. He'll probably argue. So, Lou has some selling to do.

Similar examples happen all the time at work. In fact, to go even further, nearly every day we all have to do some selling off the job as well. We try to persuade family, friends, or neighbors to accept our thinking. We may not see ourselves as selling, but that's what we're doing.

Although this book is directed mainly at people who sell for a living or who manage those who sell, it should be useful to anyone who wants to become more persuasive. For those involved directly in selling, this book has two goals:

1. To explain how salespeople can use people skills to build relationships that will improve sales results, no matter how those results are defined.
2. To explain how sales managers can use people skills to get improved sales results from their salespeople, no matter how those results are defined.

Throughout the book, we will use the terms "salesperson" and "salespeople." Your company may use the terms "account executive" or "sales representative," but we chose these words because they are widely accepted.

People Skills

"People skills" is an umbrella term for four related sets of abilities that are indispensable for maximizing sales results:

1. *Sizing-up skills.* Sales are always made to particular individuals with specific personal characteristics. When you call on a customer, you always call on someone who is unique. This person is sarcastic. That person is defensive. Still another person is genial and apparently has all day to talk.

   Sales managers are in exactly the same situation. Each of their salespeople has special characteristics, such as confidence, arrogance, insecurity, and so on.

   Whether you're a salesperson on a sales call or a sales manager in a coaching session, you want to keep some key questions in mind: What's this particular person in front of me like? What obstacles can I anticipate? Sizing-up skills help answer these questions. They help you observe the people as objectively as you can to make sense of what you see so you can pick the best way of dealing with them.

2. *Strategy-planning skills.* The difference between sizing-up skills and strategy-planning skills is the difference between a diagnosis and a prescription. Whereas sizing-up skills are for analyzing, strategy-planning skills are for determining what to do. What is the best way to deal with the other person? How can I overcome the obstacles she's likely to place in my path? How can I most effectively respond to her needs, concerns, doubts? How can I persuade her without wasting time and energy?

   Strategy-planning skills help you lay out the right plan of action for dealing with each individual. They enable you to deal flexibly with people, personalizing your approach. Your strategy for customer A will differ from your strategy for customer B or C. The same goes for each of your salespeople. Planning a strategy makes persuasion a great deal easier.

3. *Communication skills.* Once you've planned the right strategy, you'll have to get through to the other person and also find out what she thinks. Before she can be persuaded, she must understand what she's being asked to do. Before buying, a customer wants the answers to certain questions: Why should I spend money on this product or service? What will it do for me? Why should I prefer it over competitive products/services?

   Similarly, before your salespeople exert themselves to change and improve, each one wants the answers to certain questions, too: What exactly am I being asked to do? Why should I bother? What's in it for me? Responding to these questions so the answers are really understood takes communication skills.

4. *Motivation skills.* Generating understanding isn't all there is to persuasion, however. Understanding must be followed by action. When a customer says, "I see what I'm being asked to buy, but I want to think about it for six months," he may understand, but he's not committed. A salesperson who tells the boss, "I know what you mean, but I just don't see the value in doing that," may understand, but she's not committed either.

Understanding means "I get it. I catch on." Commitment means "I intend to do something about it, to follow through." Generating commitment takes motivation skills.

Are People Skills Enough?

By themselves, people skills won't produce better sales results. They're no substitute for product knowledge or good management of time and territory. However, if you have the other things it takes to produce results, technical and administrative skills and the drive to succeed, people skills can make selling more effective. They can mean the difference between success and mediocrity.

What's In It for You?

Because we said that people want to know what's in it for them before they commit, you may be asking what you will get out of reading this book. We've already said that whether you're a salesperson or a sales manager, this book will help you get better sales results. But it will help you get other results, too:

1. *Tangible results.* Whatever tangible rewards for which you are working — more money, a promotion to sales manager, a bigger district to manage, an achievement award — you'll improve your chances with people skills.
2. *Intangible results.* By using people skills, you can also get more satisfaction from your job. The ability to persuade a wider range of people should help you feel more secure, develop smoother working relationships, win new respect, and enhance your feelings of competence and accomplishment.

How It Started

How do we know people skills can do what we've said? We have seen them produce better results for thousands of salespeople and sales managers in hundreds of companies.

Our training organization, Psychological Associates, has been conducting seminars since the 1960s. As people attended these seminars, returned to their jobs, and then used their people skills, they provided a natural laboratory in which to study the effectiveness of the skills. The skills have had to be proven in real-world tests.

And they have. A whole series of follow-up studies by client companies has shown that, by and large, people skills do boost sales results and pay off as we've described. So, you can be assured that people skills are likely to help you get better results — for your company and yourself.

The Scientific Background

Where did the ideas in this book come from? And why did we believe the ideas would work?

The ideas came from psychologists, communication specialists, marketing and management specialists, and researchers in related fields. They all spent years testing the ideas. Although these researchers are too numerous to mention here, the key contributors are listed in the bibliography. By the 1960s, they had developed a large body of evidence to prove that people skills work. Of course, much more evidence has been added since that time. Follow-up studies in companies with employees who use the people skills set forth in this book only confirmed what we and most behavioral scientists already knew.

The evidence for our belief in these ideas, then, comes from two sources: the scientific community and our own experience. In the end, of course, you must judge their validity for yourself. We predict that they'll match your experience and your common sense.

People Skills Can Be Learned

Nobody is born with people skills. They are learned by people willing to expend the necessary time and energy.

This means there's nothing mysterious about people skills. They are not vague, indefinable qualities like "charm" or "magnetism." They are techniques that have been learned effectively by countless numbers of people. So, you shouldn't say, "I don't have what it takes to size up people," or "I'm not the sort of person who can motivate others." It doesn't take a special kind of person. What it takes is learning the necessary skills, practicing them, getting feedback, and then using the skills until they become second nature. This book focuses on what the skills are. Practicing and using them are up to you.

A Benchmark Profile

Before you can plan a strategy for yourself to build on your people skills, you need to size up where you are now in terms of your own sales behavior. How do you typically act during a sales call? How do you approach the potential customer? If you're a sales manager, the question becomes, how do you relate to your sales force?

We want you to complete a short profile (page 8) that should stimulate you to think about these questions. Before you start, realize that our assumption is that you are already selling or managing effectively. If you weren't, you probably wouldn't be in your present job or bothering to read this book. The profile will give you an overview of your behavior. Once you have sized up your present skills, you can begin building on them.

Complete the profile as objectively as possible. Although this profile will only give you a rough view of where you stand, the more candid you are in assigning points, the more valid it will be. The only right answers are honest ones.

When you finish this book, you may want to go back and complete the profile again. We hope the insights you gain in reading the book will give you a truer profile. That doesn't mean your first responses are worthless. They are true for how you perceive yourself right now. Complete the profile now to compare it with how you respond later. Here's how:

1. *Read each of the profile's four paragraphs.* As you do, compare them with your own behavior as a salesperson. The statements are extreme. Your own behavior may not coincide exactly with any of the statements.

2. *After reading the four paragraphs, distribute 100 points among them so that the points reflect the extent to which the paragraphs describe your behavior.* The number of points you assign to any paragraph should be proportionate to how descriptive that paragraph is of your behavior.

   For example, if you think the first paragraph describes your behavior "perfectly," whereas the others don't describe it at all, then distribute points this way: 100-0-0-0. However, this is unlikely. You'll probably see something of your behavior in several or all of the paragraphs. If so, your point distribution might look like this: 10-30-30-30 or 25-25-10-40 or 60-0-10-30. Whatever combination on which you decide is your estimate of how you sell. Be certain your total adds up to exactly 100 points.

3. *Don't assign most of your points to what you consider the ideal or best paragraph unless it really describes your behavior.* Pick the honest answer, even if it does not seem complimentary. What you want is a realistic portrait of how you interact with your customers. There are no right or wrong answers, only more descriptive or less descriptive statements.

Profile: How I Sell

First Rating | **Second Rating**

________Q1. I do most of the talking, taking a hard-driving approach with the customer. I want to get control and keep it during the encounter. I feel I know what the customer needs without my having to get much information. I'm there to make a strong impression, to show that I'm the expert. For that reason, I brush aside arguments with a barrage of facts, claims, and intimidation. I pour on the pressure to get the sale, doing what I need to overpower the customer. My job is to keep at it until the customer gives in. ________

________Q2. Rather than assert myself or set the direction of the interaction, I prefer to let the customer take the initiative. After all, he knows his own needs. Why should I get involved in his life? My job is to describe the product or service and let him make the decisions. The last thing I want is to get into an argument or be annoying. So, I go along with the customer. He'll buy when he wants to. It's foolish for me to intrude until the person is ready. ________

________Q3. My overall goal is to treat the customer in a warm, friendly way. I am eager to please, good-natured, and careful not to push or come on too strongly. I don't feel that presenting the product/service is as important as being the customer's friend. In fact, when the customer has objections, I try to gloss over them or even agree with them. It's not worth arguing if it will hurt our relationship. I figure if I go along with a customer and stay on good terms, I'll eventually get my share of orders. ________

________Q4. I try to make it clear what I expect to do for the customer. I work to discover what the customer's needs are, asking key questions and letting him do the talking. That way, I'm able to explain the product/service as a benefit to him, solving his problems or making him better off. If he has objections, I make certain I understand them and answer them to his satisfaction. I then try to summarize what the customer will gain from the purchase, clear up any doubt or confusion, and ask for the order. ________

________ **100 Total Points** | ________ **100 Total Points**

Summing It Up

Below is a form for rating your behavior. The "Q" in the tables stands for quadrant. This term will be explained in the next chapter. The top rating chart is for the profile you've just developed. The second one is for the profile you'll develop if you complete the profile again after reading the book. We urge you to complete the second rating. You'll find it instructive to compare the two ratings.

How I Sell

First Rating	Q1	Q2	Q3	Q4	
					Totals 100

Second Rating	Q1	Q2	Q3	Q4	
					Totals 100

Transfer your numerical ratings into the quadrants below to facilitate comparisons in the remainder of the book.

How I Sell

First Rating			Second Rating	
______	______		______	______
Q1	Q4		Q1	Q4
Q2	Q3		Q2	Q3
______	______		______	______
Totals 100			Totals 100	

What's Next?

In the next chapter, we introduce what will be the foundation for using relationships to sell more effectively. This is the Dimensional Model of Interactional Behavior.

CHAPTER 2

Four Patterns of Behavior

Research shows that the behavior of people when they are dealing with others usually falls within one or more of four basic patterns. This chapter describes all four, by using what we call the Dimensional Model of Interactional Behavior. It's a tool to make it easier to size up the behavior of customers and salespeople and to prescribe behavior on your part that gets results. The model is the basis for this chapter and most of this book.

What a Model Does

Like all models, the Dimensional Model is a way of organizing our observations. We constantly make observations, and our minds seem to categorize people on the basis of their behavior. We say someone is easy to get along with. Another person appears pushy to us. Still another acts friendly, and so on.

Because of this, the Dimensional Model is useful for two reasons:

1. *By systematically describing patterns of a particular kind of behavior, the model helps us understand why some interactions go well and others don't.* With this information, we can then prescribe behavior

that will improve the opportunity to make the interactions go well. Thus, it's a valuable tool for improving results.

2. *The model categorizes behavior, not people.* Putting a label on a customer or anyone else is almost certain to be misleading, because it reduces a complex human being to a mere stereotype. Moreover, people are changeable and may behave differently at different times. A label tends to be permanent. Once we categorize a customer as a "loudmouth" or a "cheapskate," we tend to dismiss him and stop recognizing that there is an intricate person behind our arbitrary label. Because we have stopped interacting with him as a person, we may cut off opportunities for communication.

The Basis for This Model

Before we get to it, you may be asking what the basis is for the Dimensional Model.

First, the model is based on empirical research. This research was originally done by psychologists in the late 1940s and 1950s. (See Appendix A for details.) Since then, many behavioral scientists have enlarged and validated that data. The Dimensional Model makes use of this research and applies it to the world of sales. We think you will see how good the "fit" is between it and your own observations of people with whom you deal. Any model that meets this test of experience is an empirical model.

Second, the model meets the test of common sense. Psychology is sometimes called "tested common sense." So, it's not surprising that most of its models verify our everyday experience. They are based on observable behavior. The Dimensional Model probably won't teach you any facts you didn't already know. It will, however, help you see those facts in a new way to derive more meaning out of what your own common sense already tells you.

The Basic Dimensional Model

We'll begin by picturing the basic Dimensional Model in Figure 1. Now, you can see why this is called a dimensional model. It is

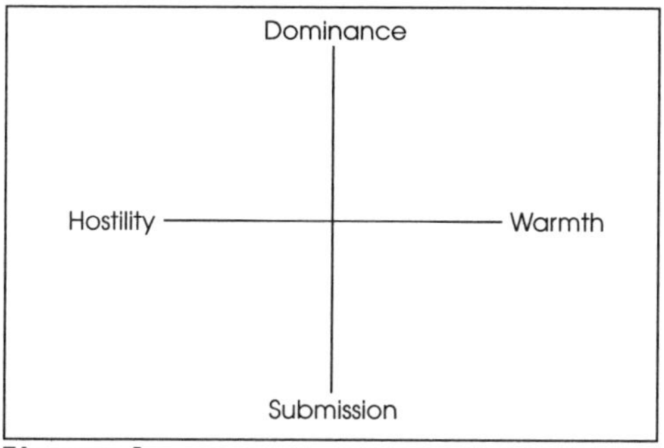

Figure 1

illustrated by two dimensions, shown as intersecting lines. Each is a continuum of behavior. One dimension is represented by dominance at one end and submission at the other. The second dimension is represented by hostility at one end and warmth at the other.

These are the four characteristics that research has found most important in explaining how people interact.

Let's define these terms, beginning with the dominance-submission dimension.

Dominance is exercising control or influence. It means being assertive, putting oneself or one's own idea forward and striving to influence the way others think or behave. People displaying dominant behavior take charge, guiding, leading, persuading, and moving other people to action.

Submission is following the lead of other people. People who act submissively are passive, reluctant to speak out. They readily give in, with little or no attempt to have influence on the course of events.

Dominant behavior tries to make things happen, whereas submissive behavior is inclined to let things happen.

Now, let's define the terms in the hostility-warmth dimension.

Hostility combines self-centeredness with a lack of regard for other people. Hostile behavior is unresponsive and insensitive to other people's needs, feelings, and ideas. It is doubtful about other people's motives and abilities. Although people displaying hostile behavior may be angry, they may or may not show their anger openly.

Warmth is concern and regard for other people, coupled with an open-minded attitude. Warm behavior is responsive and sensitive to other people's needs, feelings, and ideas. It's optimistic about other people's motives and abilities. It's possible to show warmth without being openly affectionate.

A good distinction to make is that hostile behavior is based on a negative or pessimistic view of others, whereas warm behavior is based on a positive or optimistic view. Thus, hostile people don't expect much from other people and offer little in return. Warm people approach other people at first in an open, receptive way. Hostile people see most other people as undependable, even threatening or hurtful. Warm people take a favorable view.

These four behavioral characteristics are never displayed all by themselves. They are always expressed in combination with others, and when combined, each characteristic is changed to some degree. That means the actual expression of the characteristic will differ from our definitions here.

Combining the Dimensions

Because real behavior is more complex than any one dimension, we combine the two dimensions in our model to get a more accurate view of the behavior we see around us. When we do, we come up with four basic patterns or strategies of behavior. They are: 1) dominant-hostile, 2) submissive-hostile, 3) submissive-warm, and 4) dominant-warm. This is the heart of the Dimensional Model.

Of course, there are as many different types of behaviors as there are people. Remember, these are patterns, and each pattern has innumerable variations. Within any one pattern, the behavior becomes more intense the farther it moves from the intersection.

Furthermore, as we describe these four basic patterns in terms of customers, salespeople, and sales managers, understand that no one's behavior is exactly like our descriptions. First, the descriptions are caricatures. To discuss each pattern, we have removed the shading and subtlety of real human behavior for now. Second, each of us manifests all of the behaviors to some degree at various times. No one is simply frozen in one pattern of behavior all the time.

Because the behaviors fall into the four quadrants shown in the Model, we'll call them Q1, Q2, Q3, and Q4 for short:

Q1 = dominant-hostile

Q2 = submissive-hostile

Q3 = submissive-warm

Q4 = dominant-warm.

Applying the Dimensional Model to Customer Behavior

Let's look at how the Dimensional Model can be applied to customer behavior organized around the five basic phases of the structured sales call format: opening, exploring customer needs, presenting the product/service, managing objections, and closing.

We'll describe each pattern of typical customer behavior in each phase of a sales call and the attitudes underlying the behavior. We suggest you read the model first (Figure 2, page 16) and then the explanations that follow.

Q1 Dominant-Hostile Customer Behavior

Q1 customer behavior tries to seize the initiative early in the sales call and maintain it throughout. The attitude is, "If I can fluster the salesperson, keep her on the defensive, and make her follow my game-plan, then I call the shots and make the decision on my terms, not hers."

You're dealing with Q1 behavior when the customer:

- Brags a lot, tries to impress by dropping "big" names
- Tries to monopolize the discussion
- Interrupts, listens impatiently

The Dimensional Model of Customer Behavior

Dominance

Q1 Customer Behavior

Basic premise: Keep the salesperson off-balance or you'll end up buying something you don't want or need.

Opening: Abrasive, defiant. "I dare you to sell me."

Exploring needs: Cocky, uncooperative. "I already know what I need, so why waste time talking about it?"

Presenting: Argues, interrupts. "I'll show you you're not as smart as you think."

Objections: Stubborn, belligerent, hops from objection to objection. "I'm not going to let you win."

Closing: Flatly refuses to buy or tries to dictate terms. "Don't forget who's in charge around here."

Q4 Customer Behavior

Basic premise: I expect a salesperson to explore and identify my needs and show me how to satisfy them.

Opening: Receptive, attentive. "I'm hoping to get something out of this."

Exploring needs: Candid, cooperative. "I'll answer any questions designed to further my interests."

Presenting: Attentive, inquiring. "I expect a clear, organized explanation of what I stand to gain by buying."

Objections: Straightforward, businesslike. "I won't buy until my doubts have been cleared up."

Closing: Decision based on evidence. "I'll buy if I'm persuaded it's in my interest, but not otherwise."

Hostility — Warmth

Q2 Customer Behavior

Basic premise: The less you say to a salesperson, the less chance you'll get stuck with a bad buy.

Opening: Apathetic, hard-to-read. "I don't want to encourage you."

Exploring needs: Curt, tense. "I'm not going to reveal anything you can use against me."

Presenting: Silent, indifferent. "Go ahead and say what you want — I can't stop you."

Objections: Vague, vacillating. "I'll use any excuse to avoid making a firm decision."

Closing: Gives in without conviction, makes vague commitment, or postpones decision. "I just don't feel sure."

Q3 Customer Behavior

Basic premise: I always enjoy talking to salespeople, even if I don't intend to buy anything.

Opening: Friendly, genial. "Let's relax and chat a while."

Exploring needs: Talky, highly positive. "Why spoil things by dwelling on sticky issues?"

Presenting: Agreeable, encouraging. "I don't want to ruin your presentation by being negative."

Objections: Doesn't object or does so very weakly. "I don't see any value in giving salespeople a bad time."

Closing: Makes enthusiastic purchase or alibis for not buying. "I want to preserve our good relationship."

Submission

Figure 2

- Is unreasonably stubborn and argumentative
- Offers dogmatic "I know better than you" opinions
- Reacts negatively before hearing the whole story
- Makes sarcastic or cutting comments
- Belittles you, your product, or your company
- Seems to be looking for an argument
- Claims to have all the answers
- Has a strong need to win arguments.

Q2 Submissive-Hostile Customer Behavior

Q2 behavior is defensive and safeguards against perceived exploitation. You're dealing with Q2 behavior when the customer:

- Shrinks back and says little
- Picks words very cautiously, refusing to commit himself
- Is reluctant to take even calculated risks
- Seems tense, ill at ease, or reticent
- Backs away from new ideas
- Procrastinates or responds pessimistically to most suggestions
- Shies away from discussing personal matters
- Won't deviate from routine.

Q3 Submissive-Warm Customer Behavior

Q3 is acceptance-seeking behavior. The customer works at being liked. You're dealing with Q3 behavior when the customer:

- Is mainly intent on being pleasant
- Agrees quickly and heartily, even without hearing the whole story
- Responds optimistically to most suggestions
- Is a lot more talkative than the situation calls for
- Roams illogically from topic to topic

- Seems willing to talk endlessly
- Has a good word for nearly everyone and everything
- Avoids touchy subjects
- Dodges disagreements by suggesting quick compromises
- Is easily swayed.

Q4 Dominant-Warm Customer Behavior

Q4 is pragmatic behavior. The customer tries to derive a payoff from the sales call. You're dealing with Q4 behavior when the customer:

- Is self-assured, but not cocky
- Is candid and open without being a know-it-all
- Readily defends his own ideas and listens to yours
- Acts decisively after hearing all the evidence
- Refuses to be overwhelmed by "experts"; wants to consider the facts for herself
- Asks tough but pertinent questions to help get the whole story
- Willingly takes intelligent risks when the return seems worth it
- Responds favorably or at least curiously to new ideas
- Discusses differences with an open mind
- Openly answers questions and shares information
- Doesn't mind being proven wrong.

Applying the Dimensional Model to Sales Behavior

Now we shift from customer behavior to sales behavior. The Sales Model (Figure 3) follows the same format as the Customer Model. Once again, we'll caution that our descriptions are extreme. Innumerable individual variations occur.

The Dimensional Model of Sales Behavior

Dominance

Q1 Sales Behavior

Basic premise: The surest way to make a sale is to overpower the customer.

Opening: Hard-driving, exaggerated. "The first thing to do is dazzle or intimidate the customer."

Exploring needs: Superficial. "I know what's best for the customer without asking lots of questions."

Presenting: Fires barrage of facts, exaggerations, claims, with little give-and-take. " Keep up the pressure until you wear down the customer."

Managing objections: Bulldozes, belittles, out-argues. "Bury the objection before it buries you."

Closing: Intense, overbearing. "Keep the pressure on until the customer gives in."

Q4 Sales Behavior

Basic premise: To make a sale, prove your product will make the customer better off.

Opening: Informative, results-oriented. "I tell the customer why I'm there and what I expect to do for him and find out if he's ready to work with me."

Exploring needs: Questions and analyzes. "Unless I know the customer's needs, I can't make a presentation that meets his concerns."

Presenting: Fits products to customer's needs. "I show how my product will fill his need and make him better off."

Managing objections: Patient, searching, confronts hard facts. "I try to understand and remove the customer's doubts."

Closing: Systematic, instructive, results-oriented. "I sum up final doubts, stress what's in it for the customer, and ask for the order."

Hostility — Warmth

Q2 Sales Behavior

Basic premise: You can't create sales; you can only take orders.

Opening: Mechanical, colorless. "Why knock myself out? The customer will buy when ready — in spite of anything I say."

Exploring needs: Superficial, indifferent. "If the customer needs something, he'll say it without my asking."

Presenting: Spiritless, apathetic. "I present the facts and let the customer draw his own conclusions."

Managing objections: Ignores or goes along. "I can't do much to change a customer's mind, so why try?"

Closing: Weak or non-existent. "Whether or not to buy is up to the customer. If he's ready to place an order, he'll tell me."

Q3 Sales Behavior

Basic premise: If you make yourself liked, you'll eventually make the sale.

Opening: Very sociable, relaxed, may not mention business at all. "I let the customer know I'm there for her as a friend."

Exploring needs: Superficial, unsystematic. "As long as I keep the conversation going, I'll learn the customer's needs sooner or later."

Presenting: Long-winded, unfocused. "I'm more concerned with fostering a relationship than discussing the product."

Managing objections: Agrees, glosses over, or changes topic. "Why dwell on things that could spoil our relationship?"

Closing: Weak, compliant. "I go along with the customer. As long as we're friends, I'll get my share of the business."

Submission

Figure 3

Q1 Dominant-Hostile Sales Behavior

Q1 behavior tries to power its way to results. You are observing Q1 behavior when a salesperson:

- Overwhelms the customer with facts, figures, and other "expert" opinions
- Argues even before getting the whole story
- Twists the facts to suit his own purpose
- Turns on and keeps up the pressure
- Keeps tight control of the subjects he lets the customer discuss
- Dominates or monopolizes the discussion
- Hears what he wants, disregards the rest
- Tries to convey the impression that he knows it all
- Belittles, taunts, or embarrasses the customer.

Q2 Submissive-Hostile Sales Behavior

Q2 behavior takes a fatalistic approach to selling. You're observing Q2 behavior when a salesperson:

- Makes a listless presentation, as if she's not convinced of what she's saying
- Doesn't respond to the customer, or responds mechanically
- Makes vague statements that can't be pinned down
- Backs off when the customer objects, and quickly takes "no" for an answer
- Seems tense, awkward, ill at ease
- Doesn't give evidence of hearing everything that is said
- Won't make firm commitments
- Seems dour and humorless
- Doesn't dig for information or follow up on promising clues.

Q3 Submissive-Warm Sales Behavior

A salesperson practicing Q3 behavior believes that making sales is mostly a matter of gaining acceptance. You're observing Q3 behavior when a salesperson:

- Meanders from subject to subject
- Sees only the bright side
- Agrees readily with almost anything the customer says
- Has trouble sticking to business; likes to digress
- Injects lots of upbeat phrases, like "That's terrific" or "Great," as the customer talks
- Discusses the product in general terms, but is weak on details
- Backs away from any sign of disagreement; suggests an easy compromise
- Uses far more words than necessary
- Seems to hear only cheerful information and tunes out the rest.

Q4 Dominant-Warm Sales Behavior

Q4 behavior is results-oriented and analytical. You're observing Q4 behavior when a salesperson:

- Gets the customer seriously involved in the presentation
- Listens carefully and shows she's trying to understand
- Asks lots of pertinent questions, especially about the customer's needs and objections
- Tries to discover customers' real needs rather than imposing her own ideas
- Explains how buying the product will help satisfy the customer's needs
- Comes across as a problem-solver, not a pitchman
- Adapts quickly to changes in the customer's behavior.

Applying the Dimensional Model to Sales Management Behavior

The third variation of the Dimensional Model (Figure 4) applies to managerial behavior and follows the format of the five steps to effective coaching that take place between a sales manager and a salesperson: 1) starting the session; 2) getting the salesperson's views; 3) presenting the manager's views; 4) resolving disagreements; and 5) working out an action plan. We'll explain these steps fully later.

As you go through the model, you can compare the behavior to your own, if you are a manager, or to your boss's behavior, if you are a salesperson.

Q1 Dominant-Hostile Sales Management

Q1 is coercive behavior. It relies on the sales manager's power over the salesperson. You can recognize Q1 behavior when a manager:

- Tells his salespeople what to do and how to do it without bothering to get their reactions
- Handles many tasks on his own that could easily be delegated
- Exerts tight control, even down to small details
- Uses threats, overt or implied, to get his people to do what he wants
- Makes his salespeople feel "pushed around" or "treated like children"
- Resists new ideas by belittling the salesperson who originated them, or may appropriate new ideas and pass them off as his own.

Q2 Submissive-Hostile Sales Management

Q2 behavior is pessimistic, taking a bleak view of people and their potential for change. You can recognize Q2 behavior if the manager:

- Avoids conveying her own views whenever possible, acting instead as a mouthpiece for top management

The Dimensional Model of Sales Management Behavior

Dominance

Q1 Management Behavior

Basic premise: If you want results from salespeople, run a tight ship and let them know who's boss.

Starting: Blunt, accusatory. "I let them know I'm dissatisfied and intend to straighten things out."

Getting views: Superficial or nonexistent. "I'm not interested in alibis. I know what's wrong, and I intend to spell it out."

Presenting views: Hammers away at faults. "I tell them what they're doing wrong and how to change it. That's my job."

Resolving disagreements: Squelches and suppresses. "I don't tolerate back talk."

Action-planning: Autocratic, demanding. "The point is, I want to see things done my way."

Q4 Management Behavior

Basic premise: Show your people what they'll gain by meeting their sales goals; give them an incentive to get the job done.

Starting: Candid, results-oriented. "I explain we're going to talk about pluses and minuses, so the salesperson can improve performance and meet his goals."

Getting views: Inquiring, analytic. "If I can get the salesperson to analyze his own performance, he's more likely to accept the analysis."

Presenting views: Candid, thorough, instructive. "I try to solve problems by encouraging questions and discussion."

Resolving disagreements: Explores, discusses. "I don't care whose ideas prevail as long as they're the best ideas."

Action-planning: Clear, workable. "I strive for an understanding of the plan and commitment to it."

Hostility — Warmth

Q2 Management Behavior

Basic premise: Salespeople are what they are — if you've got some good ones, you're lucky; if you haven't, you can't do much about it.

Starting: Vague, apathetic. "Coaching doesn't accomplish much, but it's something a manager is expected to do."

Getting views: Superficial, uninterested. "The more questions I ask, the more likely I'll open up problems best left closed."

Presenting views: Routine, indifferent. "I know what the company expects me to say, so I say it."

Resolving disagreements: Avoids and ignores. "Why stir up trouble? I won't change anyone's mind anyway."

Action-planning: Vague, vacillating. "Most action plans are empty talk; people go on doing what they've always done."

Q3 Management Behavior

Basic premise: If I keep morale up, I can keep performance up; a positive attitude is what counts in selling.

Starting: Cheerful, vague. "I explain that I just want to chat about how things are going."

Getting views: Talkative, unfocused. "The salesperson can say whatever he wants, but I try to skirt touchy subjects."

Presenting views: Long-winded, upbeat. "I look at the bright side. Focusing on negatives is demoralizing."

Resolving disagreements: Minimizes, glosses over, changes subject. "Arguments weaken the positive attitude I want to create. And discussing differences can lead to an argument."

Action-planning: Easygoing, compromising. "Why make strong demands? They only cause tension."

Submission

Figure 4

- Exerts little direction, unless passing along routine instructions or trying to keep things from getting out of hand when it's too late
- Puts off all but the most routine decisions
- Says little, keeping most communication superficial
- Resists new ideas by citing tradition ("Let's do it the way we always have, because that works") or by postponing a decision indefinitely ("I need to think about this some more")
- Takes things as they come, without seriously trying to motivate improved performance.

Q3 Submissive-Warm Sales Management

Q3 behavior is lenient, even indulgent, selectively emphasizing positives and playing down or overlooking negatives. You can recognize Q3 behavior when a manager:

- Sets goals that won't challenge anyone because they're easy to achieve
- Exerts little, or sometimes no, control
- Is very concerned that salespeople like his decisions
- Shares cheerful or encouraging news eagerly, while ignoring or downplaying bad or ominous news ("It will work out fine —just wait and see")
- Enjoys long, relaxed talks that focus largely on non-business issues
- Motivates by personal appeals ("Do it as a favor to me") or by cheerleading ("I know you have what it takes; go for it!").

Q4 Dominant-Warm Sales Management

Q4 behavior is realistic and pragmatic. You can recognize Q4 behavior when a manager:

- Involves her salespeople in decisions that concern them or to which they can contribute something (such as experience, insight, information, etc.)

- Delegates whenever it makes sense for the company, the salesperson, and herself
- Motivates her salespeople by helping them see what's in it for them if they meet their goals
- Involves her salespeople in businesslike discussions, asks searching questions, and listens carefully
- Tries to discuss all topics candidly, omitting nothing pertinent and including nothing distorted.

Variations in Behavior

Obviously, no one behaves the same way all the time. People act differently in different roles. Someone who uses Q1 behavior as a customer may use Q3 behavior with his boss. Even when we act in just one role, our behavior changes with circumstances. Here's why:

1. When things go well, most of us stick to the behavior we are comfortable with, our *primary* behavior. This is the standard behavior the people around us come to expect. It's a particular role that seems natural and one we use over and over again.
2. When things don't go well, out of frustration or tension, we may shift to unplanned *secondary* behaviors. These reflexive behaviors that "just happen" are usually short-lived. They explain the person under a lot of stress who suddenly "blows up," much to the surprise of others and himself.
3. At other times, we deliberately shift to another behavior in response to pressure or to attain a goal, called *mask* behavior. Think of the soft-spoken salesperson trying to meet a sales goal who "toughens up" to turn that last customer. Or the hard-nosed salesperson who isn't getting anywhere with her usual approach and tries an amiable soft-sell as a new tactic. Most masks are only worn for a short time, after which we usually revert to our primary behavior.

It's often difficult to tell whether a behavior is primary, secondary, or a mask, especially when we don't know a person. However, it really doesn't matter. As we discuss interacting with people, it's important to deal with the behavior you can see in front of you, as it occurs. Don't worry about whether it's primary or not. We'll talk more about this later.

Some Distinctions

Real-life behavior is less obvious and displayed less conspicuously than the descriptions of our four strategies. So, we want to clarify how some of the dimensions of the Model actually operate to understand the four types of behavior better.

Q1 vs. Q4 Dominance

Q1 dominance is me-centered, fueled by a powerful self-interest. It pushes one's own views, needs, and goals in spite of resistance. At the same time, it gives little consideration to anyone else's views, needs, and goals.

By contrast, Q4 dominance is us-centered. Although it still advocates one's own views, needs, and goals, it takes into account the other person's as well. While still being assertive, Q4 tries to create a win-win outcome.

Q1 vs. Q2 Hostility

Typically, Q1 hostility is more overt and more easily observed than Q2 hostility. Q1 behavior directs hostility outward. You can witness it in action when a salesperson is berated or his views are swept aside or cut off.

Q2 hostility, on the other hand, is reserved and distant. A person practicing Q2 behavior holds back showing hostile feelings and avoids being drawn into disagreement. Refusing to engage people or leaving them out of the process indicates a disdainful attitude.

Q2 vs. Q3 Submission

Q2 submission is mainly self-protective. The person gives in because standing out may get her into trouble. She feels that she is compelled to submit, rather than it being a willing act.

The purpose of Q3 submission is to foster pleasant relationships. Q3 submission is good-natured and voluntary. A person practicing Q3 behavior lets other people control her because it's a good way to gain acceptance, and it's the safe alternative to other possible responses.

Q3 vs. Q4 Warmth

Q3 warmth is more lavish. It is a demonstrated eagerness to please, characterized by a willingness to bend over backward to show goodwill and the desire to be accepted.

Q4 warmth reflects respect, concern, and responsiveness. Rather than merely pleasing someone else for the moment, a person practicing Q4 behavior tries to do what's in everyone's best interest, even if it isn't very popular.

What's Next?

Now that you know more about observing behavior in terms of the Dimensional Model, a logical question to ask is: What difference does it make? How will it help your sales to know whether a customer, your boss, or you tend to use Q1, Q2, Q3, or Q4 behavior? In other words, what's the relationship between a behavioral strategy and results? The next chapter will make that connection.

CHAPTER 3

What's the Difference?

It should be obvious by now that we favor Q4 selling. Why? Experience, research, and common sense all show that, in the long run, Q4 behavior gets better results on average than other strategies. On the whole, Q4 behavior is more effective. This is true primarily because Q4 behavior does a better job of building relationships, of creating meaningful bonds that will produce results. In this chapter, we'll demonstrate this conclusion. Whether you are a salesperson or a sales manager, Q4 skills are worth learning and knowing.

Let's start with your own experience. Whether you sell or manage, you've probably been around long enough to see all kinds of customer behavior, sales behavior, and sales results. Is there a connection between your selling behavior and results?

Based on our own experience with thousands of salespeople in our sales training courses and other research, we can state that sales results are affected significantly by particular kinds of selling behavior. Although these results cannot predict the result of any one interaction, we can say overall how results are affected. This is useful information for anyone trying to analyze her own selling, looking for every advantage.

Figure 5 shows what typically happens when each of the quadrant behaviors from the salesperson interacts with each of the quadrant behaviors on the part of the customer. As you can see, some results are average, some results are below average, and some results are above average. Specifically, there are three vital points to make while examining this chart:

1. *Q4 sales behavior, as a rule, produces above average results no matter what the customer's behavior.* This isn't true of the other sales behaviors. Q1 behavior, for example, frequently runs into trouble with customers who use Q2 behavior. Q2 behavior is very often stymied by customers who use Q1 or Q4 behavior. And Q3 sales behavior usually has a hard time with customers who use Q1 behavior. Only Q4 behavior has a high "payoff rate" with all kinds of customer behavior.
2. *The results of a sales interaction can only be explained by looking at both the salesperson's behavior and the customer's behavior.* What's critical is the interaction of the two behaviors. (Of course, we realize other factors, such as product, quality, reputation, price, service, and so forth, are crucial. Our discussion only examines behavior that makes a difference when these other factors are equal.)
3. *Q4 behavior is most likely to pay off because it answers the critical questions that usually concern customers the most.* "What's in it for me? Why should I bother listening to this salesperson? Why should I trust him? Why should I share information and ideas with him? Why should I accept his guidance and advice?" Other sales behaviors either don't answer these questions, or they answer them the wrong way. Later, for example, we'll see how other behaviors sometimes persuade the customer that he shouldn't trust the salesperson.

   Only Q4 relationship-building sales behavior consistently helps to increase trust, which results in positive answers to these questions. It provides good reasons for the customer to cooperate and buy the salesperson's product or service.

Typical Results In Salesperson–Customer Interactions

Salesperson Behavior	Customer Behavior: Q1	Customer Behavior: Q2	Customer Behavior: Q3	Customer Behavior: Q4
Q1	**Average** Scrappy, hard-hitting exchange produces mutual respect, much heat, but little understanding.	**Less than average** Customer made uneasy by fast talk and lavish claims; figures it's safer not to buy.	**More than average** Customer cannot withstand pressure and torrent of claims; "goes along" to please salesperson.	**Average** Customer made uneasy by fast talk and lavish claims; figures it's safer not to buy.
Q2	**Less than average** Customer overpowers salesperson, who quickly caves in and calls it quits.	**Average** Salesperson's low-key, undemanding manner reassures customer, who may place an order.	**Average** Salesperson's aloofness baffles customer, who may decide to "give her a break" anyway and buy.	**Less than average** Salesperson's recital generates neither understanding nor commitment.
Q3	**Less than average** Salesperson agreeably goes along with customer's objections, so customer sweeps the field.	**Average** Customer finds salesperson's warmth and refusal to pressure reassuring; may place an order.	**More than average** Both people hit it off from the start; sale seems to "come naturally."	**Average** Customer will buy if able to discern "what's in it for me" amid excessive verbiage.
Q4	**More than average** Salesperson guides customer while letting her maintain self-esteem; customer feels she can submit to guidance without "losing face."	**More than average** Salesperson quickly demonstrates trustworthiness; customer is confident of salesperson's reliability, willingly listens, and cooperates.	**More than average** Salesperson is suitably sociable, but doesn't lose sight of main objective; customer feels accepted and able to trust salesperson.	**More than average** Salesperson is businesslike and instructive; customer understands proposal and "what's in it for me."

Figure 5

Some Additional Evidence

Our conclusions about Q4 behavior are confirmed by research. Years ago, we developed a questionnaire to explore the Dimensional Model for salespeople's behavior. We asked hundreds of participants in sales management courses to think of both the "best" salesperson and the "worst" salesperson they had known, and then to identify the behaviors of each by assigning points to behaviors listed on the questionnaire.

As you can see in Figure 6, each behavior on the list was Q1, Q2, Q3, or Q4. The end result is a numerical behavioral profile. We combined and averaged the profile scores, resulting in composite portraits of the "best" and the "worst" salesperson. (Because of the scoring system, figures do not total 100.)

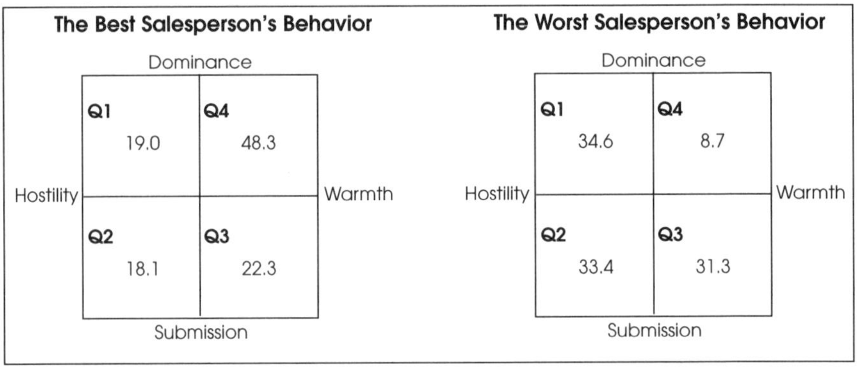

Figure 6

Two points about Figure 6 are important:

1. *In general, people see the "best" salesperson they know as someone who manifests much more Q4 behavior than any other kind.* They see the "worst" as someone who manifests much less. Q4 behavior does make a favorable impression.

2. *Just because someone is considered the "best" salesperson doesn't mean she can't become even better.* And being the "worst" doesn't mean that person is destined to stay that way. Salespeople aren't locked into their present behaviors. As we'll see, sales and managerial behavior can be changed. Interactional skills can be learned. If that weren't true, there would be no point in reading any more of this book.

Sales Management Results

If you're a sales manager, you can see similar results for management behavior in Figure 7. In the left-hand column are seven fundamental concerns of sales managers. We are interested in how each quadrant behavior affects each of those concerns. Does the behavior have a "high," "average," or "low" effect?

Our conclusions are listed, based on experience with many managers enrolled in sales management courses and from independent studies. They are generalizations, of course, but they do show a pattern.

Sales Management Behavior Results

Results	Q1	Q2	Q3	Q4
Sales results	High to average with time	Low	Low	High
Costs	High to average	High to average	High	Average to low
Morale	Low	Low	High	High
Turnover	High	Low	Low	Average
Teamwork	Low	Low	Low	High
Innovation	Low	Low	Low	High
Development of salespeople	Low	Low	Low	High

Figure 7

Conclusions

Whether you're in sales or sales management, Q4 behavior pays off best for four reasons:

1. *Q4 behavior is realistic.* Q4 relationship selling recognizes that customers want to maximize the benefit they'll derive from a purchase. It shows them how they can do it. Likewise, Q4 sales management recognizes that salespeople want to maximize the benefit they'll derive from their jobs. It also shows them how to do it.

2. *Q4 behavior demonstrates trustworthiness.* Salespeople and sales managers who behave in other ways may be trustworthy, but their behavior doesn't always convey the fact. Q4 behavior generates the trust that builds a relationship. Thus, Q4 behavior makes it plain that "You can rely on me, because I have your interests at heart as well as my own."

3. *Q4 behavior is skilled.* It doesn't just happen. Behaving in a Q4 manner takes certain skills. People who practice Q4 behavior consistently do so because they've mastered the skills.
4. *Q4 behavior is flexible.* Because one person's enlightened self-interest isn't necessarily the same as another's, Q4 behavior always tries to understand and appeal to individual interests. It tries to get past stereotypes and clichés and come to grips with the real-life person. This requires a high degree of flexibility.

What's Next?

Now that you have a basic understanding of what Q4 relationship selling is, we want to focus on why customers buy. Our next chapter gives you an organized analysis that reveals the motivations behind purchasing decisions.

CHAPTER 4

Why People Buy

Why do people buy? It's a simple question, but its answer can be very helpful in explaining what skills will be needed to get people to make a purchase. We'll describe what makes people say, "Okay, I'll sign the order." Answering this question also lays the groundwork for the chapters that follow.

Motivation and Q4 Behavior

Q4 relationship selling behavior is actually motivating behavior. A Q4 presentation does two things. First, it proves that customers will be better off buying what you're selling because their needs, both tangible and intangible, will be filled. Second, it does so in a way that satisfies certain intangible needs right at the point of the presentation.

This is what motivation is all about and why people buy. It is expressed very simply in a diagram.

Figure 8 (page 36) makes three points:

1. *Every qualified prospect has two kinds of needs,* tangible and intangible, which we'll describe.

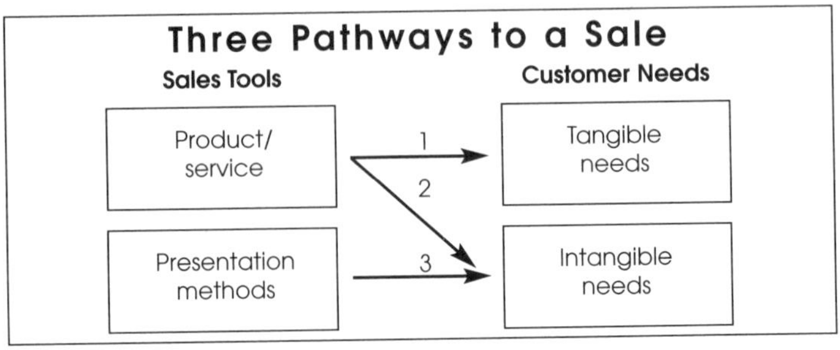

Figure 8

2. *You have the tools for filling these needs* — your product or service and your method of presentation.
3. *There are three pathways to a sale* (as shown by the arrows). The first and second are the use you make of the product or service in your presentation. If you can connect what you're selling to the customer's tangible needs (pathway 1) and to her intangible needs (pathway 2), you'll be on your way to a sale. The third pathway is the manner in which you handle the presentation. If you can connect the presentation itself — the way you interact with the customer — with her intangible needs (pathway 3), you'll be even closer to making a sale. Q4 relationship selling moves along all three pathways at once by building a relationship.

We hope to show that it isn't as difficult as it may seem to move along all three pathways. After all, in any sales presentation, you want to talk about your product or service (the "what" of the sale), and you want to arouse the customer's understanding and commitment (the "how" of the sale).

You do it by linking both the "what" and the "how" to the customer's tangible and intangible needs. Now, let's explore fully just what both of those kinds of needs are.

Tangible Needs

Tangible needs can be satisfied directly by your product or service. When a plumbing contractor has to replenish his supply of welding torches, you can satisfy his tangible need if you're selling welding equipment.

When a couple buys a house and needs fire insurance, you can fill their tangible need if you sell that kind of coverage. Tangible needs are always about something objective, something that actually exists out there in the real world, not just in the mind of the customer.

Intangible Needs

By contrast, intangible needs are always about something subjective, something that exists in the customer's mind, whether it's a feeling, an emotion, or a particular frame of mind. These can be satisfied by your product or service, but also by your method of presentation. The way you interact with the customer can fulfill an intangible need. Two examples will show how.

Example 1

Joe Hawthorne is a purchasing agent for a manufacturer looking for durable transmission belts to replace some that haven't worn well. That's a tangible need. It's also an objective need because transmission belts exist.

But Joe is tense around salespeople and especially nervous about this purchase, because he feels the salesperson maneuvered him into a bad deal the last time be bought belts. So, Joe wants to feel secure about his purchase.

That feeling is an intangible need. The confidence that he is making a good purchase exists in his head. This intangible need for a feeling of security about his purchase is subjective.

Carol Melville, a transmission belt salesperson, calls on Joe and shows him that her company's newest belt outlasts all competitive belts in laboratory tests. Obviously, her product will fill his tangible need (pathway 1). By demonstrating her product's superiority, she helps to fill Joe's intangible need for security (Pathway 2).

But Carol does something more, because she applies Q4 relationship selling. She makes her points in a deliberate, helpful way, without overstating her case or applying pressure. This helps Joe relax and not feel threatened. Thus, Carol also fills Joe's intangible need for security by her method of presentation (pathway 3) as well as with her product.

Example 2

Jenny Emerson is working at her first job since getting a business degree and wants to start an investment program that will produce some quick returns. That's a tangible need, because an investment program is something objective.

Having majored in finance at college, Jenny feels she has real investment expertise. She would like to "make a killing" on her first investment and earn admiration for her know-how. The need to be admired is real for Jenny, but it's internal, a subjective feeling. Therefore, it's an intangible need.

Furthermore, when she talks to an investment broker, she wants to be looked up to as someone who has a good understanding about investing. That's another example of the same intangible need. The feeling of being admired for her savvy can only exist in her head.

When investment broker Dave calls on Jenny, he explains a new stock issue that's likely to produce sizable returns faster than conservative investments. If Dave is right, this should fill her tangible need for quick dividends (pathway 1) and her intangible need for feeling that she's played the market like a pro (pathway 2).

Dave does something else. He asks for Jenny's ideas and opinions, listens carefully, and acknowledges her solid understanding of investing. She perceives that Dave admires her competence. So, Dave's method of presentation (pathway 3) and the service he provides fill Jenny's intangible need for respect.

The Pyramid of Needs

It's impossible to list or even categorize all the tangible needs people have. They surpass the number of all the products and services available in the world, everything from a microchip to a yacht to a foot massage to an ice cream cone.

In other words, anything that exists may fill someone's tangible need. And if enough people have a tangible need for the same product or service that doesn't yet exist, someone else will try to invent it to satisfy that need.

Intangible needs are different. They can be enumerated, and we can make helpful generalizations about them. We've listed these generalizations in Figure 9.

A Closer Look at Intangible Needs

Intangible Need	Definition	What Can Happen When The Need Is Not Filled
Self-realization needs	Needs to develop, learn, mature, make use of personal resources, increase competence and mastery, become what we're capable of becoming	Feelings of futility, alienation, bitterness, wasted chances, being at a dead end, hopelessness
Independence needs	Needs for privacy, responsibility, autonomy, self-assertion, control of our own lives and work	Feelings of frustration, entrapment, exploitation, despair, resentment
Esteem needs	Needs for recognition, reputation, status, prestige, approval, self-respect	Loss of confidence, low self-image, self-doubt, guilt, shame, resentment
Social needs	Needs for companionship, love, belonging, affection, acceptance	Loneliness, boredom, feelings of being unloved or unlovable, low self-image, estrangement
Security needs	Needs for stability, predictability, safety	Tension, anxiety, worry, fear, panic, danger

Figure 9

One design for enumerating and generalizing intangible needs is the well-known Pyramid of Needs, developed by psychologist Abraham Maslow in the 1950s. It's proven so useful that it's still widely used today. Although some psychologists would modify the pyramid in various ways, it serves to identify the intangible needs people are likely to encounter in typical interactions.

Our own slightly modified version of Maslow's pyramid is depicted in Figure 10 (page 40). The intangible needs are represented by the horizontal layers. We have added tangible needs on the diagonal to show that the two kinds of needs go together.

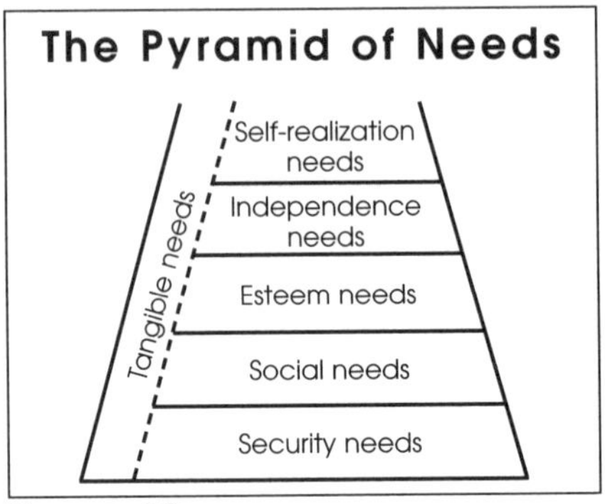

Figure 10

Why People Buy

Let's go back to our original question: Why do people buy?

People buy because they think or feel it will make them (or the organization they represent) better off. In other words, they buy when they have what they consider a good reason to buy. The reason may be rational. You actually may be able to spell it out, clearly and logically. Or it may be emotional — a gut feeling, a hunch, or a yearning. Whether the reason is rational or emotional, whether the customer thinks it or feels it, the end result is the same. The customer decides, "This purchase will produce a plus for me."

This "plus" will appear much bigger and more compelling the more the salesperson succeeds in filling both the customer's tangible and intangible needs. This is why we have examined these needs so closely. For most people, their unfilled needs, both tangible and intangible, are a minus. People buy to convert that minus into a plus — to fill in where something is lacking and create a plus. And the surest way to do that is to follow all three pathways to the sale.

This explanation makes clear what motivation is all about:

1. *People buy when they have what they consider a good reason — rational or emotional — to buy.* What's a good reason? Anything

that will make them (or their organization) better off, that represents a plus, is an incentive. People who have that incentive are motivated to buy.

2. *Whenever you give customers a reason to buy, by filling their tangible and intangible needs, you motivate them.* Motivation, then, is supplying the incentive that makes customers think or feel, "There's a plus in this for me (and my organization)."

This is why salespeople are constantly advised to sell benefits. Selling benefits means showing the customer what's in it for him if he buys. It means demonstrating to the customer's satisfaction that if he buys, he will be better off. Selling benefits is motivating.

Three Motivational Pathways

We can now see that the three pathways to a sale (Figure 8, page 36) are actually three motivational pathways. Figure 8 indicates that during any sales presentation, there are three ways to motivate the customer, that is, give her a good reason to buy:

1. You can motivate her by showing how your product or service will fill her tangible needs (pathway 1).
2. You can motivate her by showing how it will fill her intangible needs (pathway 2).
3. You can motivate her by presenting the product or service in a way that fills her intangible needs (pathway 3).

One thing that distinguishes Q4 relationship selling from other kinds is that only Q4 selling follows all three pathways. Most other selling follows only pathway 1. If the customer needs ball bearings, the salesperson tries to explain why her company's ball bearings will do the job better than any competitor's. She tries to fill the tangible needs, without giving much thought to the customer's intangible needs. Pathways 2 and 3 are usually neglected. In Q4 relationship selling, the salesperson travels down all three pathways in the same call.

Uncovering Tangible Needs

Obviously, you can't fill any needs if you don't know what they are. How do you find out? There are several ways:

1. *With little or no urging, the customer may simply tell you what the tangible need is.* For example: "We're looking for extrusion dies that'll give us a sharper definition than we're getting now." If this happens, fine. You may want to ask a few questions to determine whether this is the only tangible need, but at least you have something definite with which to work.
2. *You may have to ask about the need.* Many times, the customer won't volunteer the need. Instead, he may conceal it behind Q1 behavior ("These salespeople think they're such hotshots. Why should I be so helpful?"), Q2 behavior ("I have to be careful talking about my company with him until I know he can be trusted."), or Q3 behavior ("I enjoy chatting with salespeople who visit. We often have so much in common."). In cases like these, you'll have to ask about the need. A simple, direct question ("What are you looking for in extrusion dies?") may be all it takes.
3. *You may have to probe for the need.* Sometimes, a simple, direct question won't work, because the customer either won't know the answer or won't be certain of it. In this case, you'll have to dig by probing — asking a series of questions to clarify her thinking. We'll talk a lot about probing in a later chapter.

In any case, the important point is that tangible needs can be openly discussed. Whatever the tangible need may be, it can be talked about.

Uncovering Intangible Needs

Intangible needs can seldom be talked about, because they aren't apparent. The college graduate who wants to be admired for her smart investing will not come out and say she has this need. She won't say part of this transaction needs to bolster her esteem.

Instead, her need is buried under her behavior. What the customer says and does provides clues to intangible needs. It's indirect evidence, but it's the only evidence you're likely to get. By analyzing it, you can usually determine the customer's intangible needs.

But why go to this trouble? Don't all of us have all five of the intangible needs on the pyramid? Yes, but in each of us, one or two needs are usually more intense than the others. It's our strongest needs that we most want satisfied. These are the ones that "bother" us. Strongly-felt needs make us uncomfortable or uneasy, refusing to be ignored. So, it's the customer's strongest intangible needs that you are addressing.

What are the clues in a customer's behavior that tell you which intangible needs are most pressing, the ones creating discomfort or uneasiness? Observe what she does and how she does it. Listen not only to what she says, but also how she says it. In most cases, this behavior will reveal the customer's most pressing intangible needs. Most of a customer's behavior is verbal, not physical. So, listening is a big part of observing and analyzing a customer's intangible needs.

Our Dimensional Model provides additional insight into intangible needs. Generally, customer behavior described in the Model correlates with the intangible needs on the pyramid. There's a fairly predictable "fit" between Q1, Q2, Q3, and Q4 behaviors and certain intangible needs. The correlations are shown in Figure 11. The two broken lines leading from Q3 indicate that esteem and security needs correlate fairly closely with Q3 behavior, but not as closely as the predominant social needs.

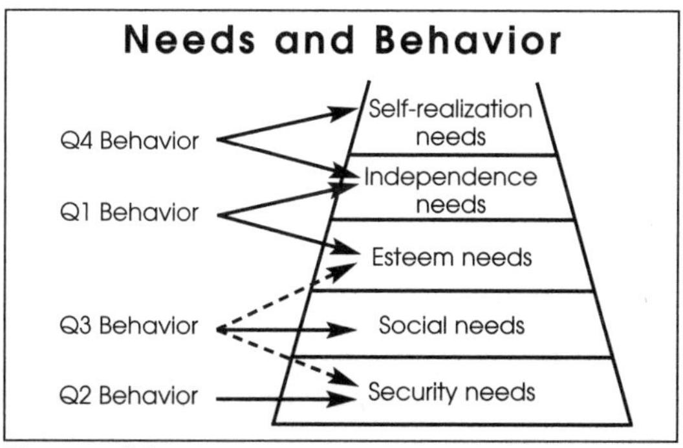

Figure 11

While Figure 11 shows the correlations, Figure 12 attempts to match customer behaviors with intangible needs (and corresponding quadrant behavior). It's certainly not infallible, because none of the behaviors is a completely reliable clue to a particular intangible need. However, it can be very helpful. When you observe a cluster of these behaviors all happening in the same interaction, it's strong evidence of a particular intangible need.

Behavioral Clues of Intangible Needs

Needs	Customer Behavior
Security (Q2)	Shrinks back. Says little. Speaks very cautiously. Won't take risks. Doesn't commit self. Procrastinates. Ill-at-ease. Leans heavily on past experience. Dislikes innovation. Pessimistic, strongly negative. Keeps discussion impersonal. Won't deviate from routine.
Social (Q3)	Outgoing, eager to please. Quick to agree. Optimistic, strongly positive. Talkative. Roams from topic to topic. Unhurried. Has good word for everybody. Quick to compromise. Has trouble making up mind. Easily swayed. Dodges touchy subjects.
Esteem (Q1) and Independence (Q1)	Brags a lot. Tries to monopolize conversation. Interrupts, listens impatiently. Stubborn, argumentative. Dogmatic. Strongly negative. Drops "big" names. Takes credit belonging to others. Likes status symbols. Hates to lose. Sarcastic. Belittles. Chip on shoulder. Has all the answers. More concerned about the short-term than the long-term.
Independence (Q4)	Self-assured, not cocky. Cooperative, yet assertive. Candid, not arrogant. Ready to defend own ideas and listen to others. Enjoys forthright give-and-take. Decisive. Reserves right to challenge the "experts."
Self-realization (Q4)	Inquiring, searching, curious, good learner. Willing to take intelligent risks. Likes innovation. Enjoys challenge. Willingly discusses differences. Doesn't mind being proven wrong. Openly shares information. Willing to experiment.

Figure 12

Two Cautions

Be aware that:

1. *In any one sales call, a customer's behavior may change as different intangible needs come into play.* A customer who is distant and hard to read at the start (Q2) may become belligerent and even abusive (Q1) later. So, deal at any given time with the behavior

you observe at that time. Deal later with the behavior you observe later. That's Q4 flexibility.

2. *A customer may show evidence of more than one intangible need at a time.* For instance, outgoing, agreeable behavior (evidence of Q3 social needs) may appear with readiness to take a chance on an unproven product (evidence of Q4 self-realization need). If that happens, deal with both needs.

The Mystery Guest

Intangible needs are the "mystery guest" at every sales presentation. Ironically, both you and the customer may be unaware of the intangible needs, but they make their presence felt nevertheless. If you can't identify them and remove the mystery, you can't deal with them. Determining the unfilled security, social, esteem, independence, or self-realization needs that are there across the desk from you is essential to successful selling. With its emphasis on making a connection with the customer, Q4 relationship selling provides a way to unmask the mystery guest and identify those needs.

If you still doubt the importance of these intangible needs, think back to all the times you've dealt effectively with the customer's tangible needs and still failed to close the sale. Assuming he had the power to place the order, isn't it likely that the reason is because you didn't deal effectively with the intangible needs? In spite of your hard work, the mystery guest "vetoed" the deal. From now on, that's something you can prevent by following all three pathways to the sale.

What's Next?

This chapter discussed at length what motivates customers to buy. Next, we will look at using the Q4 relationship skills needed to get that motivation working. How can your knowledge be used to persuade?

CHAPTER 5

Motivating Customers

Understanding why customers buy is an important step in selling. However, to persuade them to actually buy something, you have to use motivational techniques for filling their needs, turning minuses into pluses, and convincing them they'll be better off making a purchase.

These are Q4 relationship selling skills. By building a selling relationship, you don't have to pressure the customer (Q1), count on luck to make the sale (Q2), or rely on being liked (Q3). Instead, you cultivate a logical way of relating to the customer that improves your opportunity to persuade effectively.

The Motivation Process

Fully motivating a customer, that is, making him feel committed to the purchase instead of just having a lukewarm reaction, requires you to:

1. *Crystallize the customer's needs.* Get her to see that she lacks something that could make her better off. She may already know this. Your job is to make certain that she does.

As we saw in Chapter 4, crystallizing customers' needs may or may not be easy. Their needs may not be self-evident. Although some customers are willing to discuss their needs, other customers are reluctant to do so. However, we can make two safe generalizations:

- To crystallize tangible needs, you'll usually have to probe, asking questions and drawing out thoughtful, thorough answers.
- To crystallize intangible needs, you'll not only have to probe, you must also listen carefully to everything the customer says and watch her expressions, gestures, and body language. From all of this, you infer what her needs are. As we said, because customers usually don't think about or articulate their intangible needs, you must figure them out from the indirect evidence of behavior.

2. *Satisfy the customer's needs.* Show that your product or service would fill his needs, both tangible and intangible, and thereby make him better off.

   As we've said before, you have two tools for satisfying customer needs, your product or service and your method of presentation. For now, we'll talk about the first tool, your product or service, for moving you along pathway 1 and pathway 2. In a later chapter, we'll discuss improving your presentation.

Benefit Statements

How do you convince people that they will be better off buying your product or service? By using benefit statements. They are, in effect, proof statements. They provide evidence that the particular customer you're dealing with in that time and place will realize a plus if he buys from you.

A highly effective method for developing benefit statements involves the use of the *feature, function, and benefits* approach:

- Every product or service has a number of features or traits that make it unique. For example, a simple product like a felt-tip pen might have these features: an easy-grip plastic barrel, a snug-fitting plastic cap, a plastic-coated point, and so on. These characteristics make the pen the product it is.

- Every feature has one or more functions. That is, the feature exists to serve a purpose. In the case of the felt-tip pen, the easy-grip plastic barrel (a feature) makes it possible to hold the pen under all conditions without slipping out and marking up clothing (function). The snug-fitting plastic cap (feature) ensures that, when closed, the pen will not dry out or smear (function). The plastic-coated point (feature) keeps the point tapered and capable of writing with a fine line (function). Each function, then, is a reason the feature was included in the product.
- Finally, the functions of a product or service produce benefits for people who need whatever the product or service does. Suppose a construction foreman uses a felt-tip pen to write notes on a clipboard. He needs a pen he can grip firmly, because he picks it up and puts it down all day. The cap should fit tightly so the pen won't dry out or make stray marks. Perhaps, most important, he likes a pen that holds a fine point. It goes with the kind of meticulous handwriting style he uses. The pen we've described will provide all of these pluses or benefits for him.

Figure 13 (page 50) should make clearer the connection between features, functions, and benefits. Obviously, the benefits shown in Figure 13 wouldn't be benefits for everyone. They are for investors who need spendable income, a certain return, the ability to do some long-range financial planning, and a quick source of additional funds in case of emergency. Other investors with other needs might think that the features and functions we've listed don't produce any benefit at all.

The features, functions, and benefits method, then, offers this prescription:

1. *Start by crystallizing the customer's needs.* Find out what she lacks — her minuses.

2. *Describe the pertinent features and functions of your product or service.* Explain those characteristics that are relevant to her needs and what those characteristics do.

3. *Then, link those features and functions to her needs, so she sees the benefit — what's in it for her.* Prove that your product or service will convert the minuses into pluses.

An Example of Features, Functions, and Benefits

Service: Municipal Bond

Features (characteristics of service)	Functions (what those characteristics do)	Benefits (what's in it for an individual investor with $10,000 to invest)
Tax-free 6% return	Pays guaranteed rate of interest that is not liable to federal income tax.	Customer can depend on sure return, and can keep it; so the entire return becomes spendable income.
10-year maturity	Makes full amount of principal available to bondholder in 10 years.	Customer, knowing exactly how much money will be available, and when, can make long-range plans for spending it.
AAA rating	Guarantees bond will be considered good collateral for cash loans.	Customer can use bond to borrow money against in case of emergency, while investment would remain intact.

Figure 13

Why is the features, functions, and benefits concept so important? Because it makes a point that's easily overlooked: An effective sales presentation should focus not on the product or service, but on the customer.

The features, functions, and benefits approach begins with the customer and her needs. Then, it moves on to the product or service, presenting its features and functions. Finally, it returns to the customer and what benefits she'll receive from the product or service. This method reminds us of this circularity. Any discussion of the product or service must revolve around the customer.

Phrasing Benefit Statements

Although this discussion of how to phrase benefit statements is based on the features, functions, and benefits concept, we've simplified the process, boiling it down to only two steps. In practice, many salespeople ignore the distinction between features and functions and simply combine them, because they are so intertwined anyway.

The benefit statement you make should include two elements:

1. *State the customer's needs, both tangible and intangible.*
2. *Prove that your product or service will fill the needs by citing pertinent features and functions.*

We'll call this need-benefit selling. Two examples follow.

Example 1

Ted Bryan sells luggage, including sample cases to companies whose salespeople carry product samples from call to call. While exploring customer needs, Ted learns this from his customer:

"Our salespeople carry a lot of heavy steel samples around. We need sample cases that can handle the weight, so we don't have to spend a fortune replacing them every six months."

As a result, in presenting the product, Ted makes this benefit statement:

"You expressed concern about replacement costs. That's something you won't have to worry about with our case. There's a steel gridwork inside each outer wall, and tests show each wall will take up to 1,000 pounds of pressure. With this case, your replacement problems are gone, no matter how many samples your people stuff into them."

Let's analyze this exchange.

The need expressed by the customer was for cases that can handle heavy weight and don't need to be replaced often. Ted linked a feature (steel gridwork inside each outer wall) and its function (will take up to 1,000 pounds of pressure) to this need and thereby proved the benefit — the saving in money to the customer (". . . your replacement problems are gone, no matter how many samples your people stuff into them").

Example 2

Travel agent Bob Fitzgerald meets a potential customer seeking information about European tours. She is curt, argues about minor points, and makes it plain she has a low opinion of travel agents. From this behavior, Bob infers a strong Q1 need for independence. This tells Bob that the woman has a mind of her own, that she feels she knows all the answers and hates to hear advice.

Here, then, is Bob's benefit statement:

"You obviously like to be independent, to think for yourself. Our special 'Freedom Tour' will let you do just that. Once the plane touches down in Madrid, you'll be on your own for 10 days, with no obligations to the rest of the group. You can literally design your own tour, while getting the price advantage of group travel."

Here, the intangible need (for independence) was met by a feature (Freedom Tour) and function (being on your own for 10 days with no obligation to the group), which produced a strong benefit (design your own tour, while getting a price advantage).

Satisfying Needs

Figures 14 and 15 provide other examples of need-benefit selling. Figure 14 focuses on tangible needs, Figure 15 (page 54) on intangible needs. In each benefit statement, we've italicized the features and functions to show the underlying framework. In the field, you'll want to deliver full benefit statements with a statement of need followed by proof. That includes the feature, function, and any other supporting evidence, such as experience of other users, testimonials, etc. All this is then followed by a statement of what it means to the customer.

As the emphasis on product, services, and selling has become more intertwined and complex, it has become necessary for salespeople to add a third element to the benefit statement: **Prove the net gain.**

Show that your product or service will not just make the customer better off, it will also provide more value-added benefits than competing products or services.

Product	Customer Needs (voiced by customer)	Benefit Statement (features and functions in italics)
Life insurance	"Now that the twins are here, I need a lot more coverage — fast. But there's no way I can afford a fancy premium."	"You want a sizable increase in coverage, but must hold down premium payments. This *modified term plan* is the perfect answer. *All you pay for are death benefits — no cash values.* This is high payoff, low premium insurance — and the fastest way to give those twins the protection they need."
Security services	"We know we need guards on the premises. But we don't want poorly-trained people who may cause more harm than good."	"You're concerned — rightly — about having high-caliber, dependable security officers. With us, that's no problem. All our security people are *former police officers,* and they've *all been trained in the police academy.* That's a requirement for their employment. When you use our service, you're using professionals."
Word-processing equipment	"We're convinced a word-processing machine is the way to go. But we just can't afford one. All capital expenditures have been ruled out — completely — for the next year."	"You need word-processing equipment, but feel you can't afford it. Our *lease-purchase arrangement* was designed for situations like yours. You can *lease our machine for up to three years. Any time* during those three years that *you decide to buy, a percentage of the lease payments will be applied* to the purchase price. You can have your cake and eat it too."
Securities	"I don't have a lot of money to invest, so I need to be sure that whatever I do will give me a maximum net return."	"You're looking for the highest net return you can get. This municipal bond provides *a tax-exempt 6% return.* So *your net is 6%.* Your tax bracket is 50%, so this is comparable to a 12% yield on a taxable investment. This bond seems to be just what you're looking for."

Satisfying Tangible Needs

Figure 14

Sometimes, all it takes to motivate a customer to buy is a simple statement of need followed by proof of benefit. But not always. Very often, you need to prove the net gain.

Net gain is what a customer will get from buying your product or service, over and above what he would get from buying a com-

Satisfying Intangible Needs

Product	Customer Needs (inferred from customer's behavior)	Benefit Statement (features and functions in italics)
Office furniture	This customer is trying to come across as a real big shot, bragging continually about how he built his company single-handedly. (Q1 esteem need)	"We've got just the thing for an executive like you who appreciates the symbols of achievement. It's our *VIP suite,* and it's *available only in a limited edition.* You'll find this furniture in just a few top-executive offices, nowhere else."
Copying machine	This purchasing agent is unsure of himself. He keeps saying he can't afford to try anything that hasn't already proven itself many times. (Q2 security need)	"You're obviously looking for dependability. Rest assured, you'll get it with the model K-2. We've sold more of these machines to more companies than any other we manufacture. In *durability tests, it outperforms any other machine at its price.* In fact, some of our customers call the K-2 'Old Faithful' because it's so reliable."
Building maintenance services	This customer wants to please everyone. He keeps saying how unhappy people in his company are when their offices aren't cleaned properly — how bad it is for morale. (Q3 social need)	"I know how important it is to you that your people be satisfied with the condition of their offices. With our *white glove service,* you know they'll be satisfied. *If anyone in your organization complains* that her office hasn't been properly cleaned, *we guarantee to re-clean it,* that day, at no cost. That should please everyone."
Industrial chemicals	This buyer's interested in innovation. He's asking lots of questions about new developments. He seems to enjoy being on the cutting edge. (Q4 self-realization need)	"Our *double ion* etching acid is ideal for someone who appreciates technological advance as much as you do. Our lab tests show *it'll bite into plates — copper or steel — in half the time of any other acid on the market.* It does require more careful handling by your plate makers, but the savings in time make it well worth the challenge."

Figure 15

petitive product or service. Proof of net gain always involves a comparison between what you're offering to satisfy a need and what your competitors offer.

The net gain comparison might also be made over and above continuing with what a customer already has. For instance, someone with a 150-year-old Persian rug on his living room floor might be convinced of the benefits of buying new carpeting because it's easier to clean, more durable, will soundproof better, etc. Yet, she may still decide to keep what she has because, on balance, she sees more benefit from owning an antique rug than a new one. It's a status symbol, has more aesthetic appeal, and will appreciate in value.

The net gain concept is so important, you shouldn't ignore it while selling. When a customer buys from a competitor instead of from you, or when he decides not to buy but to stick with what he already has, it's usually because he thinks or feels that that's where the greatest net gain lies.

What's Needed to Prove Net Gain?

To prove net gain, you must have:

1. *A thorough knowledge of the other options, competitive or otherwise.* The more you know about competitive products or services, the better.
2. *The ability to make comparisons without belittling the other options.* Net gain selling is not "negative selling." Negative selling is more concerned with pointing out the flaws in the competitor's product than the strengths of yours.

   This is critically important. Few people want to hear that a product they're considering is a "bad" buy. If you belittle a product they were giving serious consideration, you are indirectly belittling them. To make net gain work for you, be positive.

Solution-Based Selling

An approach to selling that has gained favor in recent years is solution-based selling. It asks the salesperson to look at the bigger picture when thinking about her customer's needs. Rather than only identifying individual needs and determining how her products or services can meet them, the salesperson drills down deeper and studies the business processes of her customer. This would include making the effort to understand the customers that her customer is trying to serve.

The ultimate goal is not simply to write an order; it's to provide solutions that address the unique characteristics of her customer's business. From her in-depth analysis, she positions her products or services and tailors them in ways to provide unique benefits (solutions). Thus, finding beneficial solutions is a way of differentiating herself from the competition. If she is selling essentially the same thing as her competitor, a solution-based approach can give added value to what she is selling.

For instance, suppose you supply sand to a concrete company. Suppose also that you have quite a few competitors, and none of you has a way of distinguishing your product from the others or offering a significantly better price. In our example, sand is sand. However, you might study the way a prospective customer does business and offer "just-in-time" delivery of your sand. This means your organization can schedule deliveries of smaller quantities of sand that coincide with his production needs.

By looking beyond the direct needs your product fills (making concrete), you have found a solution for the problem a potential customer who doesn't want to tie up his money and space inventorying large piles of sand for any length of time might have. This makes you the value-added supplier in your field, offering a net gain over your competitors.

Solution-based selling is greatly enhanced by taking a Q4 relationship-building approach. What better way to understand a customer more deeply to provide solutions than to practice Q4 behavior? As you will learn, Q4 selling involves probing customers to find out as much about them as possible to serve their needs. You really get to know them and interact to provide benefits that result in a clear net gain.

The Ultimate Net Gain

In a great many cases, the ultimate net gain is you, the salesperson! This may sound like a Q3 pat on the back, but it isn't. It's a fact.

It's often very difficult for a customer to determine which option will, on balance, prove best for him. Weighing benefits against each other may not yield a clear winner. In such cases, you yourself can be the factor that tips the balance in your favor. That's because, all else being equal, customers are likely to buy from the salesperson who's most responsive to their needs.

Let's take the classic instance in which there is literally no difference between product A and product B. Securities are a good example. As far as the product is concerned, there's no difference between buying 100 shares of "Ajax preferred" from broker X or broker Y. Why, then, when selecting a broker, don't people open the telephone business directory to investment securities, and just throw a dart at the page? After all, they all sell the same product.

The answer, obviously, is that people want more than just the product. They want a broker who can provide wise investment counseling, who's concerned about their needs, who inspires confidence and trust, who's strongly committed to their welfare, and who conscientiously follows up on transactions. They want a broker with whom they feel comfortable and in whom they can confide. In this case, the broker is the net gain.

This is true for many businesses. In fact, in many companies, the salesperson is such a strong "plus" that she actually offsets a number of "minuses" in her product or service. Everyone in the sales field has heard customers say things like, "Okay, company Y offers better delivery, but I've always liked dealing with Judy, my present supplier." That's the ultimate net gain.

A Caution

Need-benefit selling won't work if the customer is not aware of his needs. In fact, if he doesn't know with which of his needs your features and functions are supposed to link up, it doesn't matter how authoritatively you present those features and functions. His reaction will probably be "So what?" A "So what?" reaction means you're in trouble.

To prevent the "So what?" reaction, always do two things:

1. *Make the customer's need explicit.* Never assume he knows what it is. Never take it for granted that, without being told, he knows with which need you're linking up. Be conversational ("You obviously want to command respect"). It's easy to spell out needs without ever using the word "need." The important thing is to make them plain to the customer and to yourself.

2. *When phrasing a benefit statement, ask yourself, "So what?".* If you were the customer sitting on the other side of the desk listening, would you really care? Would you clearly understand why it's important to you, the customer? If you can't answer yes to these questions, something's wrong. Either you haven't clearly stated the customer's need, or you haven't shown how your features and functions link up with his need. Either way, you still have some work to do.

Conclusion

Let's recall the three pathways to a sale diagram introduced in the last chapter.

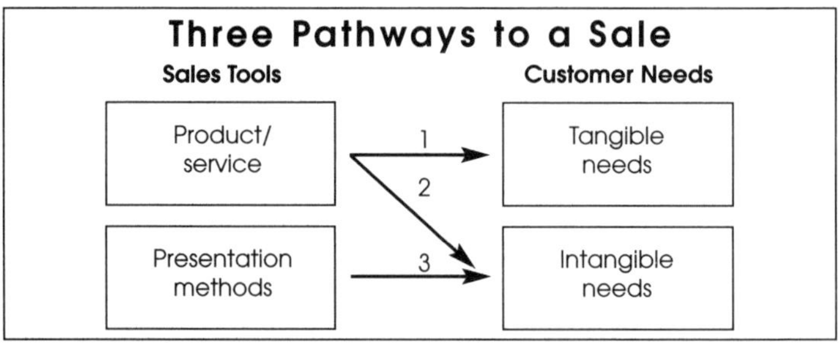

In light of what we've said about need-benefit selling, we can make two conclusions:

1. *The only way to travel pathway 1 successfully is to do need-benefit selling.* State the customer's tangible need, and then, by citing pertinent features and functions, prove that your product or service will fill it.

2. *The only way to travel pathway 2 successfully is also to do need-benefit selling,* making clear the link between your product or service and the customer's intangible need.

Need-benefit selling is the vehicle, so to speak, that will move you along both pathways smoothly, efficiently, surely.

What's Next?

You may have the greatest presentation you've ever put together all worked out and ready to deliver. But what if your customer is feeling sick? What if he's just heard some bad news? In the next chapter, we'll explore the important role that timing has in selling.

CHAPTER 6

Timing the Presentation

Here's a situation you have probably experienced. You're in a sales call, explaining the benefits of your product and feeling optimistic. Everything seems to be going great. You know almost everything about the product. You've prepared for your presentation and are feeling confident, making each of your points convincingly and enthusiastically. You have every reason to think you will make this sale.

As you wind up your discussion of benefits, you ask the customer, "Well, how does that sound?" He answers, in a lackluster voice, "I don't know. I'll have to think about it." This catches you off balance. You had expected a positive response. You quickly regain your composure and ask, "What are you unsure about?" You get the same response. You try again, saying, "Can I clear anything up?" Again, you get a lifeless response. "No. I'll think about it. If I decide to do anything, I'll give you a call."

Knowing that you're getting the brush-off, you make a few more futile attempts to find out what's bothering the customer, but you finally give up. You're bewildered, because you felt you had done everything right. Yet, the whole presentation fizzled. You will keep going over it and asking yourself what went wrong.

What probably went wrong was your timing. Even when you do everything else right in moving along pathways 1 and 2 toward your selling destination, you will not succeed if the road is blocked. And it will be blocked if it's the wrong time to try to make the sale.

Part of successful Q4 relationship selling is doing it at the right time. So, being effective will always, in part, be a matter of timing. When the customer isn't being receptive, you cannot be effective in building a relationship.

The Receptivity Predicament

In our example, what apparently happened was that while you were explaining benefits, the customer lost interest. Why? Maybe he began worrying about something and stopped paying attention to you. Perhaps, his child had telephoned right before your presentation to say she was feeling ill. Maybe he misunderstood something you said and started to fret about it, ignoring the rest of your presentation. Maybe you triggered a memory that made his mind wander. Maybe, maybe, maybe.

Any number of things might have happened, all with the same result: The customer was no longer interested. When that happens, it's the wrong time to explain benefits or anything else demanding attention and thought. No matter how forceful, eloquent, or sensible your explanation may be, it's sure to fall on deaf ears when the customer has lost interest or never had it to begin with. It's simply the wrong time.

Let's examine the dynamics of the problem.

Any time you start a sales presentation, you're presumably ready psychologically.

That's not always true of the customer. In fact, there's a good chance she's not as ready as you are. She may feel just a half-hearted interest or even less about the whole thing.

So, although from your viewpoint, the time is right for a sales presentation, from the customer's viewpoint, it may not be. Even if she's granted you an appointment and is expecting you, she may have other and more urgent things to think about. Just because you're prepared to concentrate on the presentation doesn't mean she is.

Still, you must go ahead with the presentation. If you wait for every customer to be in the right mood, you could go through entire weeks with no presentations at all. Yet, you could find that you're talking to yourself.

This is the receptivity predicament. Although you are ready for a presentation, the customer is not. Unless she's psychologically ready, that is, prepared to put herself into the presentation, you will have trouble.

What can you do to try to salvage the situation?

Because the receptivity predicament confronts every salesperson, let's define receptivity carefully.

Receptivity is the willingness to work with another person — that is, to listen attentively, consider what is said and respond constructively and candidly — to make an interaction productive.

Put another way, a customer shows high receptivity in four ways:

1. Listening carefully.
2. Considering your ideas with an open mind.
3. Responding constructively.
4. Asking useful questions.

Receptivity and Agreement

Don't mistake high receptivity for agreement. A highly receptive customer will try to understand and consider your ideas, but won't necessarily accept them. Once he has understood and considered, he may choose to accept or reject them. A highly receptive customer gives you a fair chance to make the sale. Whether you do is up to you.

This leads to a crucial point: A customer who's receptive won't necessarily be persuaded, but a customer who's not receptive is almost sure not to be persuaded. That's because persuade means to generate understanding and commitment. You cannot generate either when the other person gives no indication of being receptive.

This is one reason, if not the major reason, why so many good presentations don't work, even when they are knowledgeable, logical, clear, and benefit-oriented. Although they should produce sales, they frequently don't. As good as they are, the customers didn't really hear them. A closed and unreceptive mind doesn't give ideas a chance to sink in and make a difference. As we said, for all practical purposes, at that point you're talking to yourself.

Evaluating Receptivity

The idea that you may be talking to yourself during a presentation is hard to accept. After all, on most sales calls, the customer seems attentive. Many unreceptive customers appear open and interested, nodding their heads, making agreeable sounds, or even encouraging you. However, their appearance of tracking with you is deceiving. Their minds are actually shut off. Thus, it's important to be able to evaluate receptivity. Let's see how you can spot low receptivity in customers with the help of the Dimensional Model.

Q1 Low Receptivity

Low receptivity exhibited as Q1 behavior says to you, "I'm not going to give you a chance to get through to me. My mind is made up." It is indicated by:

1. Belligerence and flat assertions (A flat assertion is an unqualified negative comment, such as, "That product is just a piece of junk," or "You can't trust that company.")
2. Impatience
3. Interruptions
4. Sarcasm.

Q2 Low Receptivity

Low receptivity sometimes comes packaged as Q2 behavior. The message is, "I would rather not be having this conversation. It either makes me nervous or uncomfortable." It may be indicated by:

1. Silence
2. Apathy
3. Inattention
4. Nervousness.

Q3 Low Receptivity

Whereas Q2 low receptivity is mostly silent or terse, Q3 low receptivity is mostly talkative. The customer sounds receptive, but the message that comes through is, "I don't really want to settle down and concentrate on your proposal. I enjoy our conversation, but I'm not prepared to grapple with the issues of your presentation." Some indications of this are:

1. Unquestioning agreement
2. Meandering
3. Superficial questioning
4. Excessive socializing.

Many salespeople have trouble dealing with Q3 low receptivity because they don't recognize it for what it is. Although Q1 and Q2 low receptivity are readily apparent, Q3 low receptivity isn't. It seems to signal that things are going great. As a result, when the customer doesn't buy, which often happens, it comes as a shock. That's why you need to examine behavior carefully to see signs of what may really be going on.

High Receptivity

High receptivity can be recognized by Q4 behavior. It makes the point, "I'm willing to listen and cooperate. My mind is open to your ideas and presentation." These indicators are present:

1. Qualification (This term means that instead of making flat assertions, which usually signify low receptivity, the other person qualifies or tempers her remarks, usually a sign of high or rising receptivity. Instead of asserting flatly, "That's absolutely

wrong," the person qualifies her statements, showing she is giving your ideas consideration: "I'm not sure I can buy that.")

2. Thoughtful agreement
3. Involvement and non-belligerent debate
4. Pertinent questioning.

For convenience, we've summarized the signs of low and high receptivity in Figure 16.

Recognizing Levels of Receptivity	
How to Recognize Low Receptivity	
Q1 low receptivity	The customer: (1) tries to embarrass or entrap you; (2) makes flat assertions — completely negative statements ("That's absolutely crazy"); (3) shows impatience or boredom; (4) interrupts; (5) treats you sarcastically or belittles you; (6) shows anger, hostility, scorn; (7) is deliberately rude; (8) lets you know she has all the answers ("I don't need you to tell me how to run my business").
Q2 low receptivity	The customer: (1) is silent and unresponsive; (2) seems indifferent; (3) stares into space, fidgets; (4) gives non-committal answers ("Maybe," "It's hard to say"); (5) seems worried, tense, ill-at-ease.
Q3 low receptivity	The customer: (1) goes along with whatever you say; (2) shows excessive enthusiasm; (3) meanders from subject to subject; (4) asks only easy questions; (5) changes subject when an awkward topic comes up; (6) seems reluctant to settle down to business.
How to Recognize High Receptivity	
Q4 high receptivity	The customer: (1) qualifies responses ("I'm not sure I agree," instead of "That's completely wrong"); (2) voices appropriate approval; (3) gives you a chance to speak your piece; (4) asks fair, thoughtful questions; (5) discusses issues without arguing; (6) voices doubts candidly and without apologizing; (7) wants evidence for all claims.

Figure 16

Raising Receptivity

Now that you are familiar with the kinds of behavior that signal high and low receptivity, the question becomes: Is it possible to raise low receptivity? Can you penetrate that brick wall? The answer is yes.

Low receptivity isn't a permanent condition, unless you do nothing to change it. An unreceptive customer can be made receptive. How?

To better understand how to solve the problem, let's make three points about receptivity that will help in applying the remedy:

1. Many salespeople make the mistake of thinking that the surest way to get inside a closed mind is to talk their way into it. After all, selling is basically talk. If you have lots of facts and know your product, you should be able to talk persuasively enough to knock down that wall of resistance.

   That's a comforting idea, but it won't work. Remember, by definition, an unreceptive customer isn't willing to let in your ideas. Your facts, logic, and verbal skills can't help you when the customer refuses to pay attention. So, talk alone won't make a sale with an unreceptive customer. The sequence of events has to be:

   - You judge by his behavior that your prospective customer's receptivity is low.
   - At this point, rather than waste time by using facts, eloquence, or logic, you must first raise the customer's receptivity.
   - Once you have raised receptivity, you can proceed with facts and logic. Your talk is getting through.

2. We have been talking about receptivity as if it has an on or off switch. This is a simplification. Actually, a customer's receptivity can be high, low, or anywhere between. His mind is usually not completely open or closed. In fact, continuously high receptivity throughout a presentation is rare. Maintaining high receptivity requires a continuous effort by you.

3. Always expect receptivity to fluctuate. A customer's receptivity may start out high, drop down, go back up, and so on, like a roller coaster. He may shift from interest to boredom, from attentiveness to daydreaming, from cooperation to resistance. Any number of variations are possible, and they can happen in just minutes. How to gauge it?

   - Be alert to these variations. Ask yourself, repeatedly: "Where is the customer's receptivity now?"

- At the first sign of falling receptivity, move quickly to get it back up.

Probing

With this knowledge of receptivity in mind, you can raise receptivity not simply by keeping talking, but applying probing skills. These are special skills for discovering what a customer knows, thinks, or feels that will be discussed in the next chapter.

That is not to say that good probing skills will always turn low receptivity into high. No matter how hard you try, sometimes all you can do is make low receptivity a little less low. Figure 17 points out what we mean. The diagram on the left shows what you would like to achieve. You would like to take the customer's low receptivity, in this case strong Q2 behavior, and convert it to high, strong Q4 behavior. Chances are you won't succeed, because going from A to C is quite a jump during the course of a sales call.

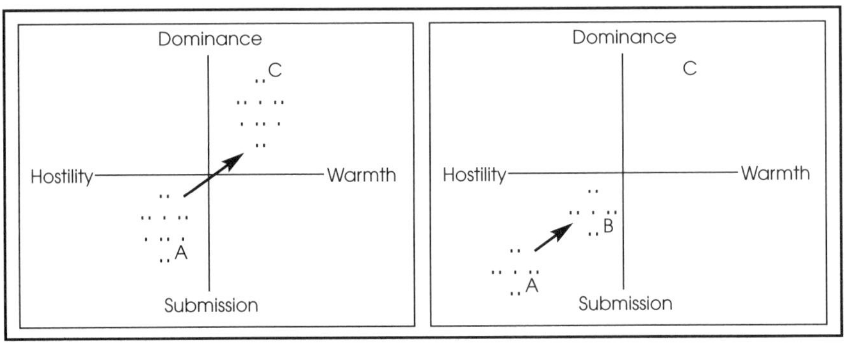

Figure 17

What you're more likely to do is shown in the diagram on the right. With diligent probing, you'll probably move the customer from A to B. Receptivity will still be low, but not quite as low. Is that change worth the effort? Certainly. The distance between A and B may look small, but it's significant. Getting a customer who's very aloof to become just somewhat aloof could mean the difference between not getting and getting the order. It's always worthwhile to raise receptivity. It's your opportunity to get your message through.

What's Next?

We hope we've made the case for raising a customer's receptivity before you try to make a sale. We said skillful probing is how you do this. So, our next chapter explains how to probe effectively.

CHAPTER 7

Probing

Remember the customer at the beginning of the last chapter? The one who lost interest in your excellent presentation? Now you realize that he must be receptive to your brilliance before you can convince him to buy. In terms of Q4 relationship selling, you won't generate understanding and commitment unless his receptivity is up. To raise receptivity and keep it there, you must be able to probe.

We believe that probing skills are essential to successful selling. That's why this entire chapter is devoted to them. Thousands of salespeople and sales managers who have taken our training seminars attest to this fact. Learning to probe has made a very real difference in their ability to do their jobs. It can make a real difference in your ability to do yours, too.

Probing and Its Functions

A probe is a technique for finding out what a customer knows, thinks, or feels. It can be used in any situation, including when a sales manager interacts with her staff members. Just as physicians use a medical probe to explore a wound, salespeople use probes as verbal tools to explore people's thinking.

Probing has two major functions:

1. *It helps you investigate what's going on in the customer's mind.*
2. *It helps you raise or sustain the customer's receptivity.*

Both these results happen simultaneously. As you explore the customer's mind, you draw him into the interaction. As you learn what his thoughts and feelings are, you transform him from someone on the other side of that brick wall who's preoccupied with his own concerns to someone willing to open up and talk about what he knows, thinks, and feels. This give-and-take—listening, responding, and getting involved—is what receptivity is all about.

Is there an easier way to raise receptivity? We can think of one: Promise the moon to the customer. Make extravagant promises about what your product or service can do. That will make receptivity soar.

The only problem is that promising miracles, even small ones, is risky business. Once you make those kind of promises, you'd better deliver. The customer won't forget your claims. So, if you can't make good on miracles, the only other way to raise receptivity is through probing.

How Probing Increases Receptivity

Probing increases receptivity by filling certain unfilled intangible needs, which we discussed in Chapter 4.

Unfilled intangible needs bother us. By creating anxiety and concern about their fulfillment, they can invade our thought processes, making us too preoccupied to concentrate on other things. This is the cause of low receptivity. We refuse to listen, not because we're stubborn or obstinate, but because we have other things on our minds, and they come first. To increase receptivity, you must clear away the customer's preoccupation. Probing helps bring her to this point.

How? By helping fill her unfilled intangible needs. As you do this, those needs nag her less, and the customer's mind is free to concentrate on your presentation.

Figure 18 shows how probing helps relieve the customer's concerns and preoccupations about the interaction. You can see that, in these cases, intangible esteem, independence, security, and social needs may nag at the customer. Probing the customer's mind to get her interacting and relating to you is reassuring and works to meet those needs head on.

How Probing Fills Intangible Needs

If the Customer's Behavior Is	His Major Personal Concern (unfilled intangible need) Is Probably	And Your Probes Should Convey This Message
Q1: belligerent, impatient, interruptive, sarcastic, negative, dogmatic	Esteem: "I'm not sure I'm going to get the respect I'm entitled to; I don't want to be taken for granted." *and* Independence: "This salesperson is going to crowd me; he'll try to run the show his way and make me conform to his ideas."	"I do respect you; that's why I'm trying to find out what you think. Your ideas matter. I don't want to shove my ideas down your throat. I want to hear your ideas, so any decisions we reach are influenced by you as well as me."
Q2: silent, indifferent, inattentive, mechanical, nervous	Security: "I don't think I'm going to like this presentation. It could prove risky. I may be pressured or outwitted and end up buying something I don't need. The whole thing could work to my disadvantage."	"I'm not trying to make trouble or to show you up. I'm giving you a chance to say what you want, in your own way and at your own pace. I may guide, but I won't push or manipulate you. I'm listening. I want to understand."
Q3: agreeable, meandering, easygoing	Sociability: "I want to come across as pleasant and likable. No matter what the outcome of the presentation, I want to come out of it knowing I'm accepted."	"I'm interested in you as a person. That's why I'm asking questions. If I weren't interested in you, I'd say what's on my mind and call it quits. Instead, I'm talking with you—not at you—proof of my interest in you as a person."

Figure 18

Finding Out What's on the Customer's Mind

Probing not only increases receptivity, it also helps you learn what's on the customer's mind. It does this by:

1. *Involving the customer.* A probe is meant to produce a response. Unless the customer simply ignores the probe, which is unlikely, he must respond in some way. Responding is involvement, the sharing of information and ideas.

2. *Eliciting information that can't be learned any other way.* If customers always volunteered their ideas and were clear about them, probing wouldn't be very important. However, many customers don't spontaneously divulge their thoughts. Probing gets customers to open up and clarify their ideas.
3. *Making the presentation matter to the customer.* A sales call may be important to you, but the customer's reaction may be "So what?" or "Who cares?" Probing makes your call matter to him by including his ideas, by letting him say what he wants to say.

   In an unspoken way, probing is also a request for assistance. By involving the customer, you are saying, "I need your participation in making this presentation. Help me do it." Feeling needed often makes people feel important, which addresses an intangible need.
4. *Venting interfering emotions.* Troublesome emotions, ranging from anger to sulking to giggling, often hinder a presentation. They lower receptivity and impair thinking. Probing eliminates or lessens them.
5. *Keeping the presentation on track.* Q4 relationship selling aims at Q4 dialogue. Trading chitchat, gossip, jokes, and war stories may all be dialogue, but not Q4 dialogue. Q4 dialogue sticks to the subject. Probing lets the customer know which topics are relevant. Every probe, in effect, says, "Let's talk about this — not something else." Probes channel the dialogue.
6. *Forcing you to listen.* Probes work on you, as well as on the customer. When you probe, you must pay attention to the response. That's because probes usually come in series, one probe paving the way for the next. You can't phrase each subsequent probe intelligently if you didn't listen to or understand each previous response.

The Eight Probes Used in Q4 Interactions

Recall the five phases of the sale: opening, exploring needs, presenting the product or service, managing objections, and closing.

For Q4 relationship selling to be effective, three things must happen in all five phases of the structured sales call format:

1. *The customer must open up.*
2. *Once she's opened up, she must keep on talking until you fully understand what's on her mind.*
3. *You must then make certain you've understood accurately.*

Probing will accomplish all three requirements throughout your selling interaction. There are eight different probes. We have grouped them to show how each facilitates one of the three functions we've just listed:

1. *Probes that open up (start the flow of information)*
   - Open-end probes
2. *Probes that keep the talk going*
   - Pauses
   - Reflective statements
   - Neutral probes
   - Brief assertions
3. *Probes that help you confirm or check your understanding*
   - Closed-end questions
   - Leading questions
   - Summary statements

We'll discuss the eight probes in this order. In each case, we'll first define the probe, then discuss its functions and explain its effect on the customer's behavior.

Probes That Open Up

Open-end Probes

Definition: An open-end probe is any question or request worded to elicit a broad response about a subject. Open-end probes coax the customer to expand on the topic in a free-ranging, comprehensive way. Because of the way they're worded, they are hard to respond to with a "yes," "no," or "maybe." They invite longer responses.

Examples:

- "Fill me in on your staff's use of telephones or pagers to keep in touch with your office."
- "What's your wish list for what you want from a copy machine?"
- "What has your reaction been to the problems with getting parts this year?"
- "What kind of security concerns do you have, now that your work force has grown?"

Notice that the open-end probe requires more than singular facts for an answer. It invites clusters of facts, plus opinions and even feelings. An open-end probe expands the discussion of a topic, rather than channeling or pinpointing it.

What open-end probes do:

- Draw out the customer, giving him a chance to answer in his own way.
- Let him know that his thinking matters to you. They improve his receptivity by communicating that his ideas are important.
- Help you come to grips with negative emotions. When you've evoked an emotional reaction, you can find out why by asking the customer, "How do you feel about that?" or "What's your reaction?"
- Help you handle flat assertions. Flat assertions are dogmatic and unqualified ("That's the dumbest product anyone ever came up with"), and they're usually exaggerated. However, they also usually contain a nugget of truth. An idea may not be the "dumbest," but it may have a serious drawback. By using open-end probes, you give the customer a chance to modify and qualify the flat assertion and isolate the nugget of truth. Here's an example:

Customer: That's the most ridiculous thing I ever heard of. That would never work here!

You: What makes you say that? *(open-end probe)*

Customer: We tried the very same kind of system years ago. It just doesn't work here. It was a disaster.

You: Tell me what happened. *(open-end probe)*

Customer: What happened was they installed the machinery, had it all set up; but, from the start, people would not use it. Nobody understood how it worked.

You: Why not? *(open-end probe)*

Customer: Because nobody from the manufacturer bothered to train anybody in our company on how to use it. The tech support people wouldn't return calls. You have to educate people if you expect them to change to a new system.

By the end of this exchange, the customer has modified his original flat assertion and explained the nugget of truth at its core. This example is a simplification: It might take many more probes to get beyond the flat assertions, but the open-end probe will get the job done.

How open-end probes affect the customer's behavior:

Q1 Open-end probes help vent Q1 anger or belligerence. They express interest in her feelings and respect for them. Thus, they begin the process of defusing their explosiveness.

Q2 Open-end probes loosen up tightlipped people. They encourage more than terse, one-word answers.

Q3 Use open-end probes sparingly when confronted by Q3 talkativeness. You'll make a bad situation worse by encouraging more meandering and wordiness.

Q4 When the customer's receptivity is Q4 — she's willing to disclose needed information candidly and fully — she must still be told what information you need. To get on track and stay on track, you can tell her *which* track with an open-end probe.

A caution: Don't contaminate your probes by including your own ideas. Saying, "I'm certain the proposal will work; what's your opinion?" is not really an open-end probe.

Probes that Keep the Talk Going

Pauses

Definition: A pause is a deliberate short break in dialogue. It's a planned silence that lets the customer collect and formulate his thoughts.

What pauses do:

- Give the customer a chance to mull over what you've said.
- Give him a chance to gather his thoughts so he can decide what to do next.
- Slow the interaction, so the customer doesn't feel pressured.
- Give you a chance to put your thoughts in order and plan ahead.
- Get reticent people to open up. Pauses create an awkward silence that the customer is tempted to fill by saying something. Most of us feel uncomfortable if the dialogue grinds to a halt for a few seconds. If the halt continues long enough, the customer will frequently try to end the discomfort by speaking out.

Pauses require discipline. You must stay quiet for as long as it takes the customer to respond.

How pauses affect customer behavior:

Q1 Q1 behavior can annoy and even anger you. If you express annoyance, you let the customer know he's irked you. Once he knows that, you'll find it harder to stay on track. Your best course, therefore, is to take the time to frame a thoughtful response you won't regret later.

Q2 Pauses help overcome withdrawn, uncommunicative Q2 behavior.

Q3 If the customer is especially talkative, use pauses sparingly. You don't need them if he already rushes to fill in pauses.

Q4 Occasional pauses give the customer time to organize his thoughts so he can present them understandably.

Finally, not every silence is a pause. We all have conversational lapses because neither person knows what to say next. The intentional pause is a controlled break in dialogue, done with purpose.

Reflective Statements

Definition: Reflective statements assert your awareness and understanding of the customer's feelings without indicating whether you agree with those feelings.

Examples:

- "I can tell you're worked up about it."
- "It's plain to me that you're bothered by this situation."
- "You're obviously happy about this."
- "You really do sound excited."

As you can see, reflective statements can mirror either positive or negative feelings.

What reflective statements do:

Reflective statements vent emotions. Venting is "letting off steam," expressing suppressed feelings. Suppressed feelings create tension that distracts us from other matters. Venting dispels these feelings and frees us to concentrate on those other matters. Here's an example:

Salesperson: Frank, how are deliveries?

Customer: (Disgustedly) Lousy, that's how. We've been completely out of inventory twice this past month. (His voice rises) I'll tell you, Dave, I'm sick of the whole situation. (Talking rapidly, obviously very agitated) Everybody's blaming me for a rotten mess that's out of my control. Your company's at fault, not me. All I get are excuses instead of merchandise. The trucker lost the shipment . . . there's a wildcat strike at the factory . . . a major piece of equipment broke down. I've had it.

Salesperson: This delivery thing's got you pretty frustrated. *(reflective statement)*

Customer: (Intensely) You're darned right it has. I've got a right to be frustrated. I'm under pressure. Real pressure. And you people are making life miserable for me. (Very angrily) Everybody's screaming at me . . . all because your company can't do its job!

Salesperson: I can tell you're exasperated. *(reflective statement)*

Customer: (A little less angry) Yeah. Everybody's jumping down my throat lately. You don't know the half of it.

Salesperson: Go ahead, Frank. I'm listening.

Let's analyze the use of reflective statements:

- Suppressed feelings are like steam building under pressure. When first voiced, they're stated with considerable intensity.
- Once suppressed feelings are expressed, the force usually builds. The emotion intensifies, just as Frank's anger did. This is called peaking. In peaking, emotions rise to a high point. This is normal, even expected, and should be permitted.
- This is where reflective statements come in. They encourage peaking, which dissipates the emotions. Once we've "gotten things out of our system," our emotions usually subside. When they do, we can discuss things reasonably, just as Frank is about to do.
- Reflective statements also tell the customer, "I know what you're feeling." Although they don't imply agreement, they show that you're an aware, responsive human being.
- Enough reflective statements should be made (combined with other probes) to vent the feelings fully. Generally, the stronger the feelings, the more reflective statements you'll need.
- What will happen if you don't let the customer vent? If his strong emotions are held back long enough, any customer will begin thinking subjectively, rigidly, and illogically. And that will make persuasion all the more difficult.

How reflective statements affect customer behavior:

Q1 Use reflective statements to vent a broad spectrum of Q1 emotions: anger, indignation, scorn, condescension, sarcasm.

Q2 Use reflective statements to vent the various forms of Q2 tension and anxiety.

Q3 Use reflective statements to dissipate positive emotions that may block the interaction. Effusiveness, inability to settle down to business, irrelevant chatter — all these can be diminished by reflective statements, such as, "You seem so wound up about this."

Q4 Even customers who use mostly Q4 behavior can get emotionally worked up. If so, use reflective statements to restore calm.

A caution: Don't agree with the customer's sentiments unless you're certain you want to. Statements such as, "I don't blame you in the least for being angry," could come back to haunt you.

Neutral Probes

Definition: A neutral probe is a question or statement that encourages the customer to elaborate on some aspect of a topic being discussed. Neutral probes have three characteristics:

1. *They ask for additional information.* They often use phrases like "Tell me more," or "Explain that further."
2. *Whereas open-end probes initiate interaction, neutral probes channel discussion of a topic, narrowing down dialogue and concentrating on just part of a subject.* Consequently, they restrict the customer in a way that open-end probes don't.
3. *They are used some time after the customer has begun to disclose his ideas and help keep the discussion going.*

Examples:

- "Fill me in on why you want to switch models."
- "Tell me more about why you feel our credit policy is unrealistic."
- "Give me the details on that packaging problem."

What neutral probes do:

- Help you get the whole story on a topic that's been only partly covered.
- Notify the customer that you're still interested in what he's saying. This keeps receptivity high.

How neutral probes affect the customer's behavior:

You can make good use of neutral probes no matter how the customer behaves. Whenever you want to know more about something that's been said, neutral probes will help.

A caution: Keep your neutral probes neutral. Don't use them to pass judgment. It's not neutral to ask, "How in the world could you like this proposal?" This question isn't a request for information. It's pushing an opinion and will likely block the flow of information back.

Brief Assertions

Definition: A brief assertion is a very short statement, question, sound, or gesture to let the customer know you're paying attention and are interested.

Examples:

Most brief assertions are statements of just several words, such as, "I see," "That's interesting," or "Okay. What else?" They can also be questions, such as, "Is that right?" "You mean it?" or "Really?" They can be brief exclamations ("Wow" or "Gee") or even just responsive sounds ("Huh!" or "Hmm"). In fact, some brief assertions are gestures, such as nodding, raising an eyebrow, smiling, or tilting the head.

What brief assertions do:

- Encourage the customer to continue with whatever she's talking about.
- Elicit additional information.
- Increase receptivity. The customer is more likely to listen to you when she knows you're listening to her.

How brief assertions affect the customer's behavior:

You can make good use of brief assertions no matter what the customer's behavior, but they're especially helpful in overcoming Q2 brevity. If the customer conveys ideas in short, uninformative packets, be patient and use a brief assertion after each response. This reinforcement will probably lead to fuller disclosure.

Some cautions: When dealing with talkative Q3 behavior, use brief assertions only when you need them. You may open the spigot wider, when it should be turned off. Also, try not to sound mechanical. Of all probes, brief assertions are the ones we use most often without thinking. If you say, "All right" or "I see" unconsciously when you don't really understand, the customer may think she has fully communicated and continue when you don't really want her to yet. Also, mechanically saying, "That's interesting," when you don't mean it may make you sound insincere.

Probes that Check Understanding

Closed-end Questions

Definition: A closed-end question is any question worded to produce a short, precise response on a restricted topic.

Examples:

There are three kinds of closed-end questions:

1. *Fact-finding questions.* These usually start with who, what, when, where, how much.
   - "With whom have you been dealing?"
   - "What time should I get there?"
   - "Where should we mail the invoice?"
2. *Commitment questions.* These seek a yes or no answer.
   - "Should we begin drop-shipments next week?"
   - "Can we settle on a 90-day billing schedule?"
   - "Do you think this program will solve the problems you mentioned?"

3. *Option questions.* These can be answered by selecting one of two or more alternatives.
   - "Would Wednesday afternoon or Thursday morning be better?"
   - "Do you want to pay with cash, check, or charge?"

What closed-end questions do:

- Help you get precise facts or opinions.
- Help you test commitment ("Yes," "Okay," "Absolutely").
- Tell you whether you're reaching for commitment too soon. For example:

Salesperson: How about it, Betty? Can I write up a truckload for you at this price? *(closed-end question)*

Customer: Hold on, Fred. Not so fast. I'm still not clear on a couple of things. I want some answers before I commit on this.

How closed-end questions affect customer behavior:

Q1 Inflated claims or commitments are typical of Q1 behavior. Use closed-end questions to test them and bring them down to earth. For example: "Is there a chance we can scale down this objective?"

Q2 Option questions are helpful in dealing with vacillation and indecision. Begin by briefly explaining the reason for the question. Then, ask it. For example: "Alice, I'm not certain I know your preference. Should I make this a priority shipment or use the normal routing?"

Q3 Closed-end questions help control Q3 meandering.

Q4 A customer whose behavior is largely Q4 will probably provide details without much prodding. Closed-end questions tell him to "focus on this."

Some cautions: Don't use a lot of closed-end questions early in the interaction. The customer may feel she's being "grilled," and that will stifle the flow of information. Usually, it's best to probe in this sequence: 1) start with open-end probes to begin disclosure; 2) follow with neutral probes to obtain more selected data; 3) use closed-end questions sparingly as you near the end of a topic.

Also, try not to use closed-end questions in rapid-fire sequence. You'll only create an interrogation effect. If you must use a number of closed-end probes in succession, always explain the reasons first.

Be careful about using closed-end probes with closed-mouth people. You may encourage more unresponsive Q2 behavior.

Leading Questions

Definition: A leading question is one that allows only one reasonable answer. The answer is implied by the way the question is worded. So, although the question may seem to give the respondent a choice, it actually leads him to the answer the questioner wants to hear.

Leading questions can be used in either a Q4 or a Q1 way. When used in a Q1 way, they're called entrapping questions, because they're designed to trap people into statements they might not make if the question were worded differently. Obviously, this can generate resentment.

When used in a Q4 way, leading questions are a legitimate means of checking your own understanding, for discussing critical issues customers have avoided or forgotten, and for moving the customer to action. They're useful for getting the customer to say something he obviously believes but hasn't yet stated.

Examples:

- "You don't want your competition to think you're falling behind, do you?" (Q1)
- "Are you suggesting you may want to switch to the deluxe service?" (Q4)
- "We haven't discussed delivery. Should we do that before we continue?" (Q4)
- "You're interested in any idea that'll put money in your pocket, aren't you?" (Q1)

- "Why don't we begin delivering to you starting next week, okay?" (Q4)

What leading questions do:

- Used in a Q4 way, they help you find out if the assumption you've built into the question is correct. They help you get agreement, but use them only after a full discussion. If you use them too early, the customer may think you're trying to force your views by putting words in his mouth.
- Used in a Q1 manner, leading questions are often nothing more than veiled threats. As such, they may backfire by fortifying the customer's resistance and lowering his receptivity. When a salesperson says to a customer, "I don't have much stock left, so you better order now; you wouldn't want to miss out, would you?" it's not really a question. The response might be, "Maybe your competitor will still have some left."

How leading questions affect customer behavior:

Q1 Q1 behavior usually implies strong needs for esteem and independence. Any leading question may be viewed as an attempt to "crowd" him. In fact, leading questions often push this customer into a dependent role, maneuvered into following your lead. With Q1 or Q4 behavior, this can be very risky.

Q2 After some discussion of a topic or issue, leading questions help overcome Q2 indecision and avoidance.

Q3 Q3 behavior, like Q2 behavior, is often reluctant to discuss certain topics and make firm decisions. Leading questions can help.

Q4 Chances are you'll use leading questions mostly as a kind of summary of what's already been agreed on with Q4 behavior. When using them, don't frustrate Q4 needs for independence and self-realization.

Some cautions: Avoid using leading questions too early in the interaction, and don't use too many of them. Of all probes, they're the most likely to be resented unless used sparingly. Use too many, and the customer may feel you're putting words in his mouth.

Summary Statements

Definition: A summary statement recaps information received from the customer. It paraphrases and condenses what you understood the customer to say.

Four points are worth noting:

1. *Summary statements differ from reflective statements.* Reflective statements mirror feelings and emotions and deal with moods or states of mind. Summary statements repeat, briefly and usually in different words, an argument or train of thought. They're not concerned with feelings, but with information, ideas, facts, opinions, and logic the customer is trying to convey.
2. *Summary statements aren't always accurate.* When you summarize, the best you can do is state the customer's ideas as you understand them. If your understanding is wrong, your summary will be wrong, too.
3. *Summary statements are the longest of all probes.* Other probes usually take a sentence or less. Summary statements may take several sentences.
4. *Summary statements don't evaluate or imply agreement.* Restating the customer's ideas doesn't mean you agree with them. In this respect, summary statements and reflective statements are alike.

In effect, a summary statement says, "This is the information you're trying to get across to me, as I understand it." That's all it says.

Examples:

- "As I understand, you think you'd be better off cancelling the purchase arrangement and going out on the open market."
- "So, you're saying you shouldn't be asked to pay full price for a shipment that arrived a week late, even if our company wasn't at fault."

What summary statements do:

- Show that you're trying to understand the customer, that you've been listening actively. This is a compliment to the customer, and it helps keep up receptivity.

- Indicate your interest in and concern for the customer. It's a powerful message to say, in effect, "I'm interested in what you've been saying."
- Let you know if you've understood or interpreted correctly. If you haven't, they signal the customer that she's not getting through.
- Bring crucial and important points into focus, while ignoring the unimportant ones.

How summary statements affect customer behavior:

Q1 Expect a barrage of disagreements and objections. To handle these, summarize the objections and then deal with them one by one. This will help you organize them into a pattern, and it will gratify the customer's esteem needs. For example:

Salesperson: "Let's see if I've got this straight, Jane. You say our billing system is messed up, our customer-service department is giving you the runaround, and I haven't been returning your calls fast enough. *(summary statement)* Is that right?"

Customer: "It certainly is."

Salesperson: "Okay. Let's talk about each point, starting with the first."

Q2 Q2 behavior seldom provides enough information to require anything more than very brief summaries.

Q3 Summary statements can help sort out the important elements of a rambling Q3 conversation. By summarizing only what seems worth summarizing, you can usually get the customer to focus on what counts. For example: "Sandy, let me try to boil this down to the essentials. As I understand it . . . ."

Q4 Even when the customer is straightforward and candid, you can't be certain you understand her unless you periodically summarize what you've heard.

Some cautions: Don't turn a summary into a speech or use it to monopolize the dialogue. Be concise. And although you should rephrase the customer's words and not say exactly what she said, don't editorialize while rewording what you understand her to have said. If you do, the summary will sound manipulative.

Probing Styles

Each pattern of sales behavior — Q1, Q2, Q3, and Q4 — has a characteristic style of probing. We have seen these styles again and again in hundreds of training seminars, where salespeople and sales managers role-play situations in which probing would be useful. From observation and study of the videotapes of these sessions, we get excellent information on probing styles. Generally, here are the patterns:

Behavior	Probing style
Q1	Mainly closed-end, leading questions, and brief assertions.
Q2	Very few probes at all. Some brief assertions or other superficial probes.
Q3	Mainly brief assertions and leading questions designed to produce positive responses.
Q4	The full range of probes.

Two points are important:

1. *Every salesperson and sales manager has a distinctive probing style, a characteristic way of soliciting information, and stimulating give-and-take.*
2. *Evidence from seminars indicates that many salespeople and sales managers have poorly developed probing skills.* In fact, four of the most useful probes (open-end probe, reflective statements, summary statements, and pauses) are actually used the least. This means that most salespeople and sales managers could dramatically increase their effectiveness by learning how to use the full range of probes. Unfortunately, some of their most helpful tools lie at the bottom of the tool box, unnoticed and untouched.

In addition, our seminars reveal a sobering fact: Before they're trained to probe, 90 percent of the salespeople never use open-end probes during role playing. Ninety-eight percent never use reflective or summary statements, and 99 percent never use pauses. These are startling figures, because in all likelihood they reflect what happens on the job as well. The list below shows the approximate usage for all eight probes observed during these seminars:

Probe	**Percentage of salespeople who use the probe**
Open-end probe	10 percent
Reflective statements	2 percent
Summary statements	2 percent
Pause	1 percent
Neutral probe	50 percent or more
Brief assertion	50 percent or more
Leading question	50 percent or more
Closed-end question	50 percent or more

The conclusion is unmistakable. Reflective statements, which are so helpful in handling emotions; summary statements, which are so useful in communicating interest and understanding; pauses, which are vital for dealing with Q2 behavior; and open-end probes, which are practically indispensable for getting customers to open up, are all ignored by most salespeople most of the time!

You, too, can ignore probes if you prefer, but you cannot ignore probes and practice Q4 relationship selling. In fact, the appropriate use of all eight probes is part of the definition of Q4 relationship selling.

Figure 19 (pages 92 and 93) provides an overview of probes and probing.

What's Next?

One of the keys to Q4 relationship selling is getting customers to feel you are on their side, that you genuinely want to fill a need by providing your product or service. To be in that position, you have to build trust, the subject of our next chapter.

Probes and Probing

Function	Probe	Definition	Characteristics	Useful in Dealing With	Cautions
Getting the customer to open up	Open-end probes	Questions or requests that get wide-ranging responses on a broad subject	Usually begin with what, why, how, tell me. Involve the customer by letting him tell what he knows or thinks.	Q2 silence: Combined with pauses, open up silent customer. Q1 negative emotions: Combined with reflective statements, vent anger and hostility.	Don't use with Q3 meandering; customer will only meander further.
Getting the customer to keep on talking	Pauses	Short silences that let the customer mull over and respond to what he's heard	Relax the pace so the customer doesn't feel pressured. Let you collect your thoughts and plan ahead. Excellent for tightlipped customers.	Q2 silence: Encourage customers to respond.	Don't end pause prematurely; let the customer break the silence.
	Reflective statements	Statements that show you know how the customer feels (without implying you agree)	Clear the air so the customer can think clearly. Vent overly negative or positive emotions.	Q1 anger: Vent bad feelings. Q2 silence: Help the customer acknowledge tension and become more responsive. Q3 exuberance: Vent high spirits.	Voice your understanding of how the customer feels, but don't voice agreement unless you're sure you want to.
	Neutral probes	Questions or statements that get the customer to expand on the topic being discussed	More focused than open-end probes. Tell the customer what further information you need.	Useful across the board. Help acquire more information and show you're listening.	Zero in on significant aspects of topic. Don't encourage talk about trivia.
	Brief assertions	Short statements that encourage the customer to keep talking	Maintain good rapport. Usually produce additional information.	Q2 terseness: Encourage the customer to amplify brief responses.	Too many of these sound mechanical or absent-minded.

Making sure you understand	Closed-end questions	Questions worded to produce short, precise answers	Excellent for getting final commitment and gathering details.	Q3 meandering: Focus on specifics and control roaming. All others: Help you learn details and fill in gaps.	Watch out for the "interrogation effect."
	Leading questions	Questions that suggest their own answers	Excellent for getting the customer to commit. Check your understanding by telling you whether the assumption built into the question is correct.	Q2 and Q3 indecision: Use late in the discussion to guide and move the customer to action.	Use sparingly, or the customer will think you're trying to trap him.
	Summary statements	Statements that summarize information obtained from the customer	Focus on facts, not emotions. Help the customer clarify his own thinking by hearing it summed up by you.	Q1 multiple disagreements: Summarize, then deal with them one by one. Gratify customer's esteem by showing you're listening. Q3 confusion: Focus on relevant facts. Separate the wheat from the chaff.	Don't put words in the customer's mouth; summarize what you heard, not what you wanted to hear.

Figure 19

CHAPTER 8
Building Trust

Let's recall that the sales presentation in Q4 relationship selling is distinguished from that in any other kind of selling because it follows all three pathways to a sale at one time.

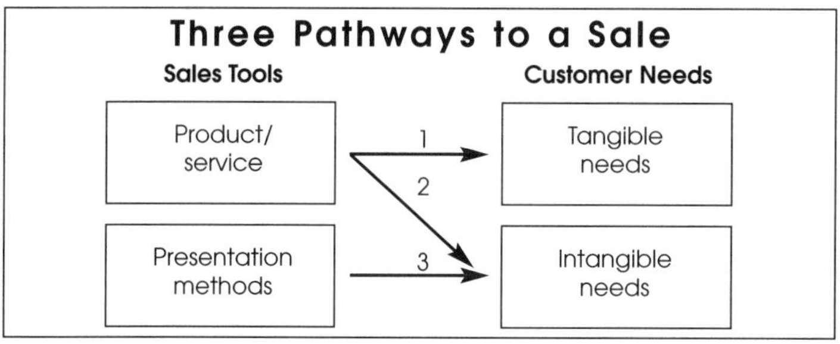

Three Pathways to a Sale

So far, we've concentrated on the skills needed to move along pathways 1 and 2:

1. *Motivational skills* — instrumental for selling benefits, showing the customer she'll be better off buying your product or service.
2. *Sizing-up skills* — help you determine what needs your customer has, particularly intangible ones.
3. *Timing skills* — helpful because to have a chance at convincing a customer she'll be better off, her receptivity must be high.

4. *Probing skills* — essential for crystallizing the customer's needs and raising receptivity.

If need-benefit selling is the vehicle that takes you along pathways 1 and 2, then these skills are what propels the vehicle along those roads.

In this chapter, we'll see that these same Q4 skills are equally important for moving forward along pathway 3. They can be used to remove or get around the barriers that so often stand between the salesperson and the close.

What barriers? Skepticism, doubt, uncertainty, indecision . . . which can all be grouped under one label: lack of trust. Q4 presentation methods that use these four skills are used to build trust. In this chapter, we'll see how.

Persuasion and Trust

Trust is the conviction held by the customer that you want to make her better off. It's the feeling that "You're on my side. So, I know you won't take advantage of me, or mislead me. I'm confident you won't advance your interest at my expense. If you win, I win too."

Obviously, trust hinges on honesty. But the sad fact is that many completely honest salespeople don't convey trustworthiness. Many are highly competent but never realize their full potential because they don't come across as trustworthy.

The more people trust you, the more readily they'll believe you. The more readily they believe you, the more easily you'll generate understanding and commitment. That's what persuasion is all about. When there's little or no trust, your chances of persuading the customer are very poor. This simple fact has enormous consequences in selling. It's not good enough to *be* honest and trustworthy. You must also *convey* that honesty and trustworthiness.

The best way to demonstrate trustworthiness is by using Q4 behavior. Q4 behavior evokes trust because it is:

1. *Responsive.* It shows an interest in and concern for the customer's needs, ideas, and feelings.

2. *Attentive.* It puts the customer at the center of the presentation and makes everything else revolve around his needs.
3. *Constructively candid.* It speaks out without blame, editing, or censoring, telling the whole story.

Thus, the basic message of Q4 relationship selling is "I'm here to make you better off." That's not usually the message delivered by Q1, Q2, or Q3 behavior.

Q1 Selling

You've no doubt dealt with "hotshot" salespeople who make wonderful-sounding, but unsubstantiated, claims. They insist they have all the answers but seldom bother to ask questions, and they pressure hard for an order. What has your reaction been? Chances are you felt suspicious and guarded. Even if these salespeople are completely trustworthy, they generate mistrust.

Q2 Selling

You've probably known salespeople who just go through the motions. They are lackluster performers who don't have their hearts in what they're doing. What was your reaction? Because they didn't seem convinced themselves of their presentation, you probably felt uncomfortable and guarded. These salespeople may also be trustworthy, but they generate doubts.

Q3 Selling

Finally, you've probably dealt from time to time with easygoing salespeople who are genial, talkative, and consistently positive. How did you react? Chances are you felt skeptical and maybe uneasy at getting what seemed to be just one side of the story. These "nice" salespeople may be completely trustworthy, but they very often generate apprehension.

Mistrust, doubt, apprehension — they all diminish the salesperson's reliability in the eyes of the customer. A salesperson who deserves trust may not be trusted, not because his intentions are bad, but because his behavior doesn't convey the message that he'll act in the customer's best interest.

Presentation Barriers

A presentation barrier is anything a customer says or does that slows down, sidetracks, or permanently stops the presentation. That's not to say that customers erect barriers based always on something the salesperson says or does. A customer may erect a barrier for reasons that have nothing to do with the salesperson. For instance, she may be preoccupied by something. A preoccupation barrier isn't the salesperson's fault.

Nevertheless, a great many barriers are reactions to something the salesperson says or does that triggers mistrust, doubt, or apprehension. They're responses to Q1, Q2, or Q3 sales behavior. Let's see how this happens.

Barriers Raised by Q1 Selling

The basic message of Q1 selling is: "I know what's best for you, and I'll prove it to you — or make you buy it anyway!" This message is conveyed by characteristic Q1 behavior: high pressuring, knocking competitors, interrogating, pushing ahead when receptivity is low, boasting, making unsupported claims, or interrupting.

As a result, the customer frequently sets up these presentation barriers to stop the attack and maybe even force a retreat:

1. *Open antagonism.* The customer may meet the salesperson's claims with undisguised Q1 hostility.
2. *Withdrawal.* The customer may use Q2 behavior, freezing up and refusing to cooperate.
3. *Suspicion.* At the very least, the customer is likely to become skeptical and wary.
4. *Capitulation.* Of course, the customer may give in, being flattened into submission. However, understanding and commitment may be low, and that means a barrier will already be in place for the next call. Repeat business may prove impossible.

All these barriers are evidence of mistrust. They're erected because the customer doesn't dare place much confidence in the salesperson. So, she's unwilling either to confide in or believe her.

Barriers Raised by Q2 Selling

The basic message of Q2 selling is "I'm not strong enough to influence you. So, I won't try. I can only explain my product to you and hope for the best." The message is conveyed by characteristic Q2 behavior: seemingly being detached, failing to confront objections, wavering when asked for a firm commitment, not bothering with benefit statements, and making a generally lackluster presentation. All this leads to building these customer barriers:

1. *Uncertainty.* The customer starts feeling uneasy.
2. *Disrespect.* The customer may look down on the salesperson.
3. *Annoyance.* The customer may feel irritated because the presentation is so perfunctory.
4. *Lack of understanding.* The worst barrier of all may be that the customer doesn't see any reason to buy.

All these barriers are evidence of doubt. They're erected for one reason: The salesperson seems so unsure and so unconvinced, the customer in turn feels unsure and unconvinced. The customer may not be openly mistrustful or disbelieving, but he is doubtful.

Barriers Raised By Q3 Selling

The basic message of Q3 selling is "Let's relax, and get to know one another. Once we establish a good personal relationship, we can get around to talking about my product or service. After all, what could be more natural than doing business with a friend?"

This message is conveyed by characteristic Q3 behavior: taking an upbeat approach to everything, failing to mention touchy business problems, digressing frequently, compromising quickly to avoid arguments, and sometimes even "giving away the store." All this leads to raising these customer barriers:

1. *Disrespect.* The customer gets the impression the salesperson is soft — unable to stand up for herself.
2. *Skepticism.* As the salesperson dodges or glosses over one sticky topic after another, the customer wonders, "Am I getting the whole story? Is she holding something back?"

3. *Seizure of control.* Vexed by the salesperson's slow-moving, rambling tactics, the customer may take over the presentation.
4. *Lack of understanding.* Because her needs haven't been thoroughly probed, the customer can't fully understand what's in it for her.

A Q3 presentation is long on generalities, but short on details. The customer is expected to buy on faith, not evidence. As a result, she's not really sure why she should buy, and she's certainly not committed to the idea.

All these barriers are behavioral roadblocks put up by the customer. They impede, or even halt, the presentation by substituting mistrust, doubt, or apprehension for openness and high receptivity.

Are they inevitable? Certainly not. The salesperson can behave so that the customer has no reason to put up barriers. That's one thing that distinguishes Q4 from other sales behaviors. It gives the customer no reason to be mistrustful, doubtful, or apprehensive. If the customer does put up barriers during a Q4 presentation, it's not because of anything the salesperson has done.

Q4 Relationship Selling Behavior and Guidelines

One of the fundamental reasons that Q4 relationship building gives you such an advantage is that it's a trustworthy selling behavior. A Q4 approach is the best way to keep the customer from raising the barriers we've discussed. And if the customer starts out with barriers already in place, building a Q4 relationship is your best opportunity to overcome them. In fact, it may be your only chance to replace them with trust, understanding, and commitment.

How can you use Q4 selling behavior to demonstrate your trustworthiness, allowing you to move on to generate understanding and commitment? By combining the skills we singled out — sizing up, timing, probing, and motivating. The rest of this chapter presents 15 guidelines for putting these skills to work for you.

They are all ways to keep customers from raising barriers or to overcome barriers once they are raised.

1. Become Aware of Your Behavior

Before you do anything else, try to discover what you're doing now that might undermine trust.

On sales calls, ask yourself if you use Q1 behavior. Do you blame, judge, warn, demand, counter-argue, or interrogate?

Do you use Q2 behavior? Do you evade hard issues, show indifference, or withdraw?

Do you use Q3 behavior? Do you smooth over differences, digress, or compromise quickly?

Don't answer glibly. Think back over your experience. Look closely at your behavior on recent calls. Candidly and objectively determine whether you're doing anything now that might create mistrust and how it could be changed.

2. Search Out Feedback

Even your best effort may not produce candid answers about your behavior. Like most of us, you probably judge yourself by your intentions, whereas your customers judge you by your actions. That's why feedback from other people is often so important in gaining self-awareness. If you can, search out feedback from your co-workers. Ask your boss or fellow salespeople whose candor and judgment you respect how they would answer the three questions about you. (Do I use Q1 behavior? Do I use Q2 behavior? Do I use Q3 behavior?) Include the three questions in customer satisfaction surveys. Once you know, you can take steps to change your behavior.

3. Make Every Call a Trust-builder

Show concern for the customer's needs, ideas and feelings on every call you make. Whether on a sales call, follow-up call, or a call to discuss a complaint or handle a problem, probe to uncover any needs you might fill. If the customer has called you with a complaint, for example, don't walk in and immediately tell him how you intend to handle it. Investigate the complaint first. Make sure you fully understand it. See whether there are any other needs or problems with which you might help. Build your image as a problem-solver, someone who's there in the customer's best interest.

4. Listen at a Thinking Level

You can't build trust unless you pay attention to the customer. Trust requires listening at a thinking level, to hear what the customer really thinks and feels. To do this, ask yourself, "Do I really get what she's saying? Do I know why she's saying it? Do I understand how this relates to everything else she's said?"

Two probes will help test your understanding. First, use summary statements, which restate what you think the customer has said. If she agrees, fine. If not, probe to clarify her meaning. Second, when the customer is expressing strong feelings, use reflective statements to determine whether you are really picking up her emotions correctly.

If you've listened closely and still don't understand, tell the customer, and then probe. Summary statements combined with neutral probes will help. For example: "I'm not sure I understand, Alice. As I understand it, you say you've got the budget for this order, but you still can't afford it. Tell me more about that."

5. Maintain Two-Way Involvement

It's hard to trust anyone who does all the talking. Any monologue is likely to create mistrust. After all, a monologue usually dwells on your interests, not those of the customer. And if you seem neglectful of his interests, why should he trust you?

This may strike you as unrealistic. Your objection may be "When I talk to a customer, there are certain things about which I must talk, whether he's interested or not. If I have to talk about warehousing, that's what I have to do, even if he'd rather talk about something else." This is valid. It points to why you must do two things:

1. *Start the discussion with a benefit statement, to motivate the customer.* Get the customer to understand that it's to his advantage to talk about warehousing, that he'll get something from it.

2. *Probe throughout.* This is the most dependable way of creating and maintaining two-way involvement. It's also the only way to make certain you're getting through. Probes provide the feedback that tell you whether you're just talking to yourself.

Another good way to maintain involvement is to reward the customer psychologically for staying involved. Psychological "payoffs" stimulate further involvement. You can make these payoffs in several ways:

1. *Express appreciation for and, if possible, approval of the customer's ideas.*
2. *Show interest.* An occasional nod of the head or other brief assertions can help. Keep your eyes on the customer.
3. *Ask for the customer's opinions.* From his viewpoint, exchanging views is psychologically rewarding. It proves you're interested.
4. *Use reflective and summary statements.* These show understanding, and that's rewarding.

Psychological payoffs are important. Without them, the customer may get the idea you're not interested. If you're not, there's no reason to trust you.

6. Demonstrate Interest and Understanding

If your customer ever starts feeling that you are not interested or don't understand her, she will quickly feel there's no reason to trust you.

Interest and understanding are not the same thing. Interest shows that you want to know what something means to the customer. Understanding demonstrates that your interest has paid off, that you know what something means to the customer. Put another way, interest is your *attempt to* understand what a customer means, whereas understanding is when you actually *do* understand. To demonstrate either, probe.

Five probes are especially useful for demonstrating interest: open-end probes, pauses, neutral probes, brief assertions, and closed-end questions.

Two probes are especially useful for demonstrating understanding: reflective statements and summary statements.

Remember, to build trust, it isn't enough to be interested and to understand. You must demonstrate your interest and understanding. Then, you, yourself, become a benefit to the customer. That's the ultimate Q4 achievement.

7. Prove You're Open-Minded

This is another way of saying don't use Q1 behavior. Don't come into the presentation committed to just one line of thought. Don't take for granted you know what's best for the customer. If you do, your behavior is almost certain to raise the barriers of antagonism, withdrawal, and suspicion.

One way to show that your mind is open is to probe. Not the superficial Q2 kind of probing that merely skims the surface ("How's your inventory today?") without being willing to dig into serious concerns. Not the irrelevant Q3 probing, which may ask dozens of questions, but only on "safe" or extraneous subjects ("How are your kids?").

When we say open-minded probing, we mean Q4 probing that focuses on pertinent topics — whether pleasant or unpleasant — probes them in depth, and then draws conclusions.

Even Q4 probing, however, may not be enough to convince the customer you're open-minded. You may be required to change your mind. After all, if you probe skillfully and uncover evidence that disproves your original point, but then still insist on sticking to that point, the customer will probably conclude that your probes were insincere. Unless you change or modify your thinking in the light of contrary evidence, you'll come across as glib, but closed-minded.

8. Create a Problem-solving, Solutions-based Climate

A customer with an unfilled need obviously has a problem. Because Q4 relationship selling fills those needs by developing solutions, it might be called problem-solving. Solving a customer's problem is one of the surest ways to build trust. It's also very difficult to do if you don't first create the right climate, one in which the customer admits she has a problem (an unfilled need) and seeks your help in solving it.

How can you get the customer to admit the existence of a problem? By raising her receptivity, probing, and then analyzing her needs, as described in Chapter 4. Once you do that, she'll probably acknowledge the problem and seek your help. Why? Because she'll trust you. You're the one who has crystallized her unfilled needs.

So, don't tell the customer she has a problem. Help her see it for herself. Bring her to the point at which she realizes and acknowledges it. That will produce a trusting, problem-solving climate in which you can do some Q4 benefit-selling.

9. Create an Advice-seeking Climate

If simply telling the customer he has a problem invites mistrust, so does giving him advice when his receptivity is down. Unsolicited advice usually suffers the fate of anything else offered when receptivity is low. It's unlikely to be considered or accepted.

Instead, you'll first have to increase receptivity. Then, probe to get him to think about his uncertainty. Once he admits he is not certain, he will find it easier to seek your advice. Having established a high level of receptivity, you can give the advice. As always, however, make certain he understands what is in it for him.

10. Keep Receptivity High

The previous guideline made the point, once again, that we can't stress enough: Your trust-building efforts will prove futile if you don't work to keep receptivity up.

Never assume that high receptivity will stay that way. It fluctuates and will only stay high if you work at it. Stay alert to signs, whether Q1, Q2, or Q3, that receptivity is drooping. If it is, probe to bring it back up. Remember that the customer's low receptivity may be a sign that your own behavior has lapsed into Q1, Q2, or Q3. One good way to keep your own behavior Q4 is to be alert to signals that receptivity is declining.

In working to keep receptivity up, remember that the need-benefit equation can do much to maintain receptivity. When a customer is aware of her needs and sees the connection between them and your presentation, it's not very likely her receptivity will decline much.

11. Face Objections and Troubled Emotions

This is one of the most difficult of all Q4 practices. When a customer sees you refuse to face harsh facts, it creates mistrust. The problem is that evasion is a very tempting way to get through a sales call when trouble arises. From time to time, every salesperson is tempted to ignore an objection, disregard an embarrassing question, or smooth over an angry outburst. From time to time, every salesperson would like to change the subject, pretend he didn't hear, pass off an objection with a joke, or otherwise stifle a customer.

All we can say is, don't do it! When you neglect a customer's concerns, you convey one of two messages: "I don't care about your concern" or "I'm too weak to do anything about it." Either way, you sow the seeds of doubt or mistrust. In Chapter 7's discussion about reflective statements, we explained how to deal with troublesome emotions. In Chapter 10, we'll explain how to manage objections. The point is that when building trust, you must face up to objections and troublesome emotions.

12. Try to Close Only When Receptivity Is High

Chapter 10 deals with closing techniques, which we will discuss fully. For now, however, we want to make this important point: Rushing the close and trying to lock up the order when the customer's receptivity is down is a common cause of mistrust. It reinforces Q1 and Q2 stereotypes such as: "Salespeople will do anything to get an order," and "When you talk to a salesperson, watch out! You'll get stuck with something you don't need."

We're not saying you can't make sales when receptivity is low. High-pressure tactics will work sometimes. People don't always make decisions with full understanding and commitment. But even if you can close when receptivity is low, it is no way to build trust. You may get the order this time, but you may not even get your foot in the door next time. That one-time customer may steer clear of you in the future. If you're interested in building trust for the long haul, try to close only when receptivity is high.

13. Show Respect at Every Point

Respect and trust are two sides of the same coin. Even if we have strong security or social needs, we all want respect. We all also find it difficult to trust someone who talks down to us and makes us feel foolish or inadequate. We tend to trust people who respect us and mistrust people who don't.

Although it's easy but risky to score points off someone with strong Q1 esteem needs ("Tom, you've got a real romance going with yourself"), the consequences are predictable. They will usually answer back right then and there. You may have a struggle on your hands.

In contrast, customers with Q2 or Q3 needs don't usually answer back, although their behavior can easily provoke us into showing disrespect without our realizing it. They sit and "take it," suppressing their resentment. This suppressed resentment, however, may come back to haunt you, either as subtle sabotage or as heightened apathy. Understand that scoring points at a customer's expense will drive down receptivity, build mistrust, and make persuasion much harder.

14. Sell Net Gain, Not Net Loss

A net gain presentation focuses on the superiority of your product or service. A net loss presentation focuses on the inferiority of a competitor's product or service.

A net gain presentation draws factual comparisons between your solution to the customer's problem and other potential solutions. A net loss presentation tears down the other solutions. As many salespeople have learned to their regret, knocking the competition is a good way to build mistrust. To generate trust, stick to factual, restrained comparisons between products or services.

15. Create a Win-win Situation

Win-lose struggles with customers are obviously no way to build trust. They take the attitude that the customer is an opponent and only one of you can walk away with a victory during a sale. Once a customer discovers that it's you vs. him, he'll consider you an adversary, very difficult to trust.

Another problem with win-lose struggles is that they generate high emotion, which makes it hard to think rationally. It's basic human psychology that the more emotional we get, the less clearly we think. For instance, it is very difficult to think logically when we're angry. Generally, the more intense the anger, the more jumbled the thinking. Clear thinking requires making sound inferences and drawing sound conclusions from them.

We're not cautioning against Q4 discussion. A spirited give-and-take in which you and the customer explore alternatives, find flaws in each, and try to pick the best alternative is good when it is problem-oriented. In contrast, Q1 quarreling is ego-oriented and degenerates into personal attacks. Barbed remarks, sarcasm, and bad tempers make it very difficult to build trust.

What's Next?

Although trust establishes ideal conditions for understanding and commitment to flourish, it doesn't guarantee they will. You have to work at achieving them. The next chapter shows specifically how to build understanding and commitment during your presentation.

CHAPTER 9

Building Understanding and Commitment

Building trust creates for you the opportunity to persuade the customer. It makes him receptive to your presentation, as you move along pathway 3. But trust alone isn't enough.

To get your customer to see what's in it for him, that is, to fill his needs, you must also build understanding and commitment. You must convince him that "what's in it" for him is really worth having. So much so, in fact, that he's ready and willing to buy.

A customer may trust you completely and have a need for your product or service, but still not understand why he should buy from you. This can happen for many reasons: Your presentation may be poorly organized, your arguments may be illogical, your language may be unclear, your explanations may be too technical, and so on.

To build understanding and commitment, you draw on the same basic sets of Q4 skills for building trust: sizing-up, timing, probing, and motivational skills. With these skills, there are guidelines to keep in mind during your presentation that will build understanding and commitment.

Fit Your Words to the Customer

Nothing sinks receptivity faster than the wrong word or words. And when receptivity sinks, understanding and commitment sink with it. What makes certain words wrong with a particular customer? Beware of three kinds of words that aren't suitable:

1. *Words that conflict with the customer's intangible needs.* Words can create adverse reactions when they clash with a customer's intangible needs. For example, a customer with strong esteem and independence needs (Q1) may be annoyed by hearing you say, "Just follow my instructions to the letter, and you won't go wrong" or "Before committing yourself, maybe you'd better run it by your boss."

   These statements sound harmless enough, but they collide with this customer's needs. After all, she wants to be number one, not number two. So, any statement that emphasizes following, rather than leading, is likely to lower her receptivity.

   Statements such as these could easily trouble a customer with strong security needs (Q2): "Here's a real challenge — a chance to do something nobody's tried before" or "Yes, it's a risk; but if it works, you'll be a hero."

   There's nothing wrong with these remarks. They're just not likely to appeal to a customer who wants serenity, who would rather merge into the background than make people "sit up and take notice" of her.

   Some statements will unsettle a customer with strong social needs (Q3), such as: "This decision may not win you any friends; but, believe me, it makes sense anyway" or "So what if you do get a few complaints from your employees? You'll still be saving money." Imagine saying these things to a customer who's especially eager to be accepted.

   The best rule is: Don't say anything that will clash with the customer's strongest intangible needs. With a little effort, all these examples could be rephrased so the idea is retained, but the threat is removed.

2. *Words that are negative or offensive.* Although we may feel justified in thinking a customer is being pigheaded, close-minded, or a loudmouth, using those words in trying to persuade her will guarantee a drop in receptivity and may lose the sale.

   If you must talk about her stubbornness, use less loaded terms. Tell her that although you appreciate firmness and sticking to principles, she needs to see your proposition in a broader, more flexible way. You can approach and deal with her "close-minded" attitude without using words that create a negative reaction.

3. *Other words that are inappropriate.* These include offensive words that are insulting. Sexist words or racial references should not be used. Be careful about using obscenities around people who may be offended. The best rule is: If you think a word may offend, find a better one. Why run the risk?

   Also, avoid inside language, such as slang, buzz words, or jargon, that may fail to communicate or may annoy customers. Don't use pretentious words that are designed to show off your vocabulary. When you do, you are needlessly putting distance between you and your customer.

Say What You Mean

Sometimes, in an attempt not to seem too blunt or emphatic, we obscure our meaning. However, when you disguise your ideas, you can't expect customers to recognize them. Particularly, watch out for:

1. *Soft words.* These are words that are used in place of harsher-sounding words to cushion reality. For instance, "downsize" is often used to replace the blunter sound of "terminate" or "fire." But it doesn't help to say, "There's been a suspension in the fulfillment area," when you need to tell a customer that his order wasn't shipped on time. Deal with the fact rather than tiptoe around it.

   Much is made these days of "politically correct" wording. This is the use of soft words to avoid offending someone. Try to leave no doubt about your meaning. You don't have to be brutal or offensive, but your meaning should be direct and communicate clearly.

2. *Unclear analogies.* We often lace our conversations with analogies, comparing one thing to another. Sports analogies are a fairly common way to make comparisons for customers, because they draw on broadly shared experiences.

   However, analogies are sometimes used to evade or water down what you really want to communicate. Does it help build understanding to launch into a comparison of your customer with a mountain climber? Rather than going off on a comparison that obscures what you want to communicate, say it more directly.

3. *Vague language.* The less specific you are in choosing words to get your point across, the greater the chance of misunderstanding. If a customer wants to know when a new product will be available and you say, "Soon," he may think you mean next week, when you actually mean in a month or two. It's obvious the misunderstanding that will occur if you leave it at that.

   When you use language that is too abstract, you weaken the effect of what you say and work against understanding. "Our new printing process is faster than it was and is easy on the wallet" says something generally positive. However, it doesn't begin to tell the customer what's in it for him if the salesperson could be saying the process is 30 percent faster for four-color printing and can save as much as 25 percent in costs in the first six months of use over the old system.

   These specific statements will stick with the customer and can be used as an objective measure for comparison in the days, and even weeks, to come.

Space Your Ideas

When you want to explain a complex subject or get across a large amount of information, do it in small clusters.

First, convey a small amount of information. Then, check to see if it's understood. Clarify or amplify when necessary. Get the customer's reaction. Discuss it when necessary. Convey a little more information. Finally, repeat the cycle until you've covered the whole topic. Spacing ideas is important for two reasons:

1. *Ideas are easier to digest a few at a time.* When you bunch ideas, the customer is expected to absorb them all at once, but that's difficult. We all have trouble soaking up large doses of information at one time.
2. *Many customers, especially those with strong security needs (Q2), feel threatened by a barrage of ideas.* These fears drive down receptivity.

The best rule is to present your ideas with appropriate pauses between them. You'll stand a better chance of being understood.

Be Alert to Differences in Interpretation

What you want the customer to hear and what the customer actually does hear are frequently two different things. One reason is that the customer may inflate what you tell him, deflate it, or erase it.

Inflation

Customers with strong needs for esteem (Q1), security (Q2), or acceptance (Q3) may inflate what they hear by making it more emphatic or more definite than you intended.

For example, you may say to the customer, "That's not a bad idea." He hears you as saying, "That's a great idea." Or you say, "I'm not certain my firm will go along with your idea. I'll have to check." His behavior changes from that point on, because he decides from what you said that you have turned him down.

You can cut down on inflation by probing. Ask the customer to summarize what he's heard. That will tell you whether he's inflating it. If he is, you can repeat your original message.

Deflation

When deflating, the customer makes your ideas less emphatic or less definite than you intended.

For instance, you tell him you have the best model on the market. Later in your conversation, he quotes you as saying your model is good. You say prices are certain to rise in September. When the price question comes up a bit later, he refers to what you said about prices possibly going up sometime this Fall.

You can detect deflation by probing.

Erasure

The customer may hear you but feel so uncomfortable by what you say that he wipes out the message. He may not remember hearing it at all, or he may convince himself he heard it wrong. For example, if you tell a customer with strong social needs (Q3), "A lot of people are going to be very unhappy to hear how you feel," he may become upset. He may assure himself with the thought that you didn't really say what he thought you did. He may eventually believe you never said it. For all practical purposes, your words will be erased.

The same could happen if you tell a customer with strong esteem needs (Q1), "You really made a bad buy. In fact, I think somebody put one over on you."

Obviously, if a customer chooses to erase your words, you can't stop it. During the presentation, however, you can ask him to summarize what you've said, so you're at least certain he heard it. He'll find it harder to forget something he's repeated out loud.

Use First-person Statements

Q4 relationship selling is marked by willingness to confront sensitive problems and resolve them to the satisfaction of both the customer and the salesperson. Obviously, this is seldom easy. After all, many of the touchiest problems involve the customer, and pointing a finger at her will usually make the problem worse.

How, then, can you confront a problem by meeting it head-on, openly and candidly, without antagonizing or upsetting the customer? By using first-person statements.

When you include yourself in a statement about a problem, you are saying, in effect, that you are implicated in the situation along with the listener. A first-person statement begins by focusing on "I" or "me," that is, the salesperson. The focus may later shift, but initially you are saying, "Look, I'm right in the middle of this thing." Here are some first-person opening statements used as ways of bringing up a problem:

- "I'm having trouble understanding . . . ."
- "I'm worried about . . . ."
- "Something puzzles me . . . ."
- "I seem to be overlooking something . . . ."

First-person statements share four traits:

1. *They describe the customer behavior that you, the salesperson, are in some way concerned or troubled about without passing judgment on it*. They merely say what it is.
2. *They describe your feelings about the behavior, still without passing judgment.*
3. *They describe the possible consequences of the behavior.*
4. *They ask for the customer's help in solving the problem.*

Contrast these with second-person statements, which focus on "you" the listener, not "I" or "me," the speaker. Some typical second-person openings are:

- "You shouldn't say things like that."
- "You'd be better off if . . . ."
- "Why do you insist . . . ?"
- "You ought to . . . ."

All second-person statements say or imply that something about the customer or his behavior is wrong or undesirable. They're fault-finding statements.

Second-person statements also single out the customer. The word "you" makes it plain that the fault is the customer's and implies that the speaker is blameless.

The differences between several second- and first-person statements is show in Figure 20.

Second- vs. First-person Statements

Second-person	First-person
Your bookkeeping department is running late on payments.	I'm worried about your payments running late, because our credit department might start insisting on C.O.D. shipments. That means I won't be able to give you the kind of service you deserve. What can we do to stop that?
You didn't keep your word.	I'm in an embarrassing spot. I expected your order in July, so I told my boss it was certain. Now he feels I misled him. Can you tell me what happened so I won't make the same mistake again?
You're driving our shipping department crazy.	I got some worrisome news yesterday. Our shipping department is unhappy because three straight deliveries have been turned back at your receiving dock for lack of space. So, they say that if it happens again, they'll tack on a $50 reshipment fee, and that'll run your costs up. Got any ideas how we can prevent that?

Figure 20

Whereas each of the second-person statements simply points the finger of blame or disapproval at the customer, each of the first-person statements acknowledges the existence of a problem, makes the point that both salesperson and customer are involved in the problem, and looks for solutions.

First-person statements open up a Q4 relationship approach to problem-solving. They keep communication open, minimize defensive or retaliatory behavior by the customer, and make him part of the problem-solving process. Customers may not enjoy hearing first-person statements, but they're more likely to be receptive to them than to accusatory second-person statements.

Use Process Checks When Necessary

Every salesperson knows the helpless feeling that comes from being completely baffled during a presentation. You think to yourself, "We're going around in circles," or "This is hopeless; I just can't get this customer to settle down and talk business," or "I may as well call it quits; nothing I say seems to satisfy this guy."

This can happen even when you follow all the guidelines we've laid out so far. Human nature virtually dictates that sometimes, despite your Q4 efforts, you cannot increase receptivity or get the customer involved and cooperating. When this happens, a process check can be very effective.

A process check is a special type of first-person statement. It does three things:

1. *It summarizes without judging the breakdown in the process that you are having.*
2. *It uses the first-person* ("I" or "we").
3. *It requests the customer's help in solving the breakdown.* It does this with an open-end probe.

Here are some examples:

- "Beth, we seem to be fighting an undeclared war. What can we do to declare a truce and start working on the same side?"
- "It looks like we're taking off in different directions, Jeff. How can we get on track and stay there?"
- "Joe, tell me what I might have done that's made you reluctant to discuss this."

Let's examine these statements.

They're called process checks because they say, in effect, "Something seems wrong with the process, the way we're interacting. Let's see what we can do about it."

It makes sense to implicate both people in the problem. After all, it takes two to interact. If the interaction isn't going well, both people share responsibility.

Process checks don't blame the customer. A statement like, "Ray, you're doing everything you can to sidetrack this discussion, and I think it's time to stop it," is not a process check. A process check admits that you're both involved, without assigning blame. It asks for help in solving the problem, without putting the whole burden on the customer.

Do process checks always work? No, but they work more often than you might think. They're a classic form of Q4 behavior because they're assertive and constructive, candid, and solution-oriented.

What's Next?

We talked about the five phases of a sale in earlier chapters. Now that you know about the skills and tools needed to conduct a true Q4 presentation, we want to examine how to apply them to structure sales calls as we move an account through the Sales Cycle.

CHAPTER 10

Planning the Sale

Now, we can put it all together! You are now aware of the skills and guidelines needed to generate trust, understanding, and commitment. You recognize what it means to practice Q4 relationship selling and what it will take to make it work effectively for you. It's time to apply that understanding to structuring any sales call. Structuring provides a framework that is the spine of Q4 relationship selling.

The Sales Cycle

It has frequently been said that 80 percent of achieving success can be attributed to planning. To plan a sales call, a successful salesperson must establish where the account is in the Sales Cycle to set attainable sales call objectives. The Sales Cycle is composed of five stages:

1. Suspect
2. Prospect
3. Potential Buyer
4. Buyer
5. Client.

These stages serve as a process model for planning sales call objectives and tracking sales progress. The objective of selling is to move suspects through the cycle as far as possible, until they ultimately become either a buyer or a client. By using the organization of the sales cycle, salespeople can establish reasonable commitments that their contacts may make in each stage, thereby advancing toward the sale in stages.

The time required to move through the sales cycle varies with the complexity of the sales process in each industry. Both the starting point within the cycle and the final achievable stage also vary by company and industry. Companies selling new products in expanding markets, for example, normally begin at the suspect stage. The beginning point for businesses selling to industries in mature markets may be at the potential buyer stage, because all suppliers and buyers know each other, and all buyers have been qualified. Knowing how long it takes to move an account through the cycle enables a salesperson to:

- Plan and set specific sales call objectives at each stage
- Maintain a record of sales progress
- Forecast with greater accuracy when sales will occur.

The suspect is defined as a contact who has come to you as a lead or inquiry and may have a need for your product or service. Your first objective in the suspect stage is to qualify the contact to determine whether the person wants to buy now. In addition, you can generate interest, gain the suspect's trust, and begin building a relationship during this stage. You want the contact to disclose needs and to commit to the continuation of the sales process.

The prospect is a contact who has divulged a general need for your product or service. In other words, the contact has been qualified and meets your qualifying standards. Your objectives in the prospect stage are to explore, clarify, educate, create, and prioritize the contact's specific needs. Again, you want a commitment from the contact to continue the sales process, which, in this stage, ultimately leads to the contact's consent to see your sales presentation.

With a potential buyer, you have confirmed the need for specific products, services, or solutions that he will purchase from you or the competition. Your objective in the potential buyer stage is to sell by presenting value-added benefits and net gain, managing objections, and closing. The commitment you want from the contact in this stage is to carry on the process until the purchase is made.

In the buyer stage, the contact has recently agreed to purchase your product, service, or solution. Your objective in this stage is to implement the product or service solution. This may include delivery, installation, training, follow-up, and servicing the account. Here, you are working toward the commitment of continued business and looking toward the possibility of becoming the buyer's sole supplier.

A client is a customer who has purchased your products, services, or solutions and is thoroughly satisfied. Your objective in the client stage is to build a solid business relationship. As that relationship develops, you open up a host of commitment possibilities, such as becoming the client's sole supplier or participating in joint ventures to develop product and service solutions that are mutually beneficial to both parties.

In summary, your success can be greatly enhanced by understanding the sales cycle. You will plan and strategize better, because you'll know where to begin in the sales cycle and how far you can reasonably progress through the cycle with each sales call you make.

The Components of Structuring the Sale

Moving a targeted account through the sales cycle requires a series of well-planned and well-executed structured sales calls. The number of sales calls needed to move a suspect to buyer or client are generally placed in one of two categories, either short- or long-cycle sales. A short-cycle sale can consist of as few as one or two calls. Short-cycle sales are simple and involve few decision-makers. Long-cycle sales are complex sales that may take many calls in a long period, and involve multiple decision makers. In any case, consistent success in a short- or long-cycle sale depends on well-planned and well-conducted structured sales calls.

Phases of the Structured Sales Call Format are opening, exploring customer needs, presenting the product or service, managing objections, and closing. These phases are a customized format that can be applied to any successful interaction; later we'll describe parallel phases that sales managers can use to coach salespeople or for nearly every kind of manager-employee interaction.

For now, we can apply all the knowledge you've gained to explain the structuring that leads to a successful sale. In this chapter, we'll talk about how it works when encountering any kind of customer. In Chapter 11, we'll specify how to tailor this format to fit specific Q1, Q2, Q3, and Q4 customer behaviors.

As we explore the details, don't lose sight of the outline of this chapter — an examination of each component, one by one.

Pre-call Planning

In the last decade, the salesperson's role has rapidly changed, becoming a more demanding one. Vast amounts of valuable prospect and customer information can be accumulated in seconds from company web sites. Orders, requests for information, assistance, and daily communications can be transmitted instantly. A salesperson is expected to know his contact, customer, or affiliate's business so well that he is often considered to be a vital part of the company's operation. Customers want the salesperson to be a vigilant contributor, who is constantly developing new approaches and innovations to make their companies more successful. A successful salesperson who wants to use Q4 relationship selling must use the pre-call planning period to learn his contact's business and the competitors' offerings, and be prepared to apply problem-solving expertise to that business.

Open the Sales Call

The sales call refers to any call made on a prospect or customer to advance a sale, now or in the future.

Every Q4 opening tries to:

1. *Set the right tone.* Make the customer feel confident and at ease.
2. *Arouse interest and attention.* Explain the purpose of the call, and persuade the customer that it's worth her while to concentrate on it.
3. *Get the customer involved.* Set a pattern of active, instead of passive, participation so that the customer is speaking up and contributing.
4. *Check the customer's receptivity.* Find out whether she's ready to cooperate in making the call pay off for both of you.

Here's how a Q4 opening is conducted:

1. *Extend a Q4 greeting, and be suitably sociable.* A Q4 greeting is confident and cordial. Beyond that, the key word is "suitably." Obviously, you want to establish rapport with the customer, but you want to do it without wasting time or annoying her. This means you must find the right "sociability level."

   If she's inclined to use Q3 behavior, you'll have to loosen up and engage in a little extra small talk. If she's inclined to use Q2 behavior, you can cut down on the small talk. And if she's inclined to use Q1 or Q4 behavior and get down to business quickly, you'll obviously want to do the same. It's impossible to generalize about how much sociability is the right amount. Use your sizing-up skills to gauge the customer's behavior.
2. *Explain why you're there.* Once you are past the small talk, tell the customer what your purpose is explicitly. "I was in the neighborhood and just thought I'd drop by" is not a statement of purpose. It's saying you have no purpose. The customer's entitled to know what the call is all about. Spell it out.
3. *Explain what the customer stands to gain.* As soon as you explain why you're there, raise receptivity immediately by coupling your purpose for being there with a tentative benefit statement. What will she get out of your call? Because you haven't probed the customer's needs yet, the benefit can only be tentative at this stage, but making the attempt is still worthwhile.

Here are two examples:

- "Mr. Kent, I'm here to demonstrate our new fastening machine *(purpose)*. There's a good chance you can use it to eliminate one whole step from your assembly operation and cut down on your assembly costs *(benefit)*."
- "Miss Davis, I'd like to get some financial information from you *(purpose)*. Once I've got it, there's a strong possibility we can set up an estate plan that will give you tax advantages you don't now enjoy *(benefit)*."

4. *Probe receptivity.* The opening is supposed to lead into the exploration of needs. You hope your benefit statement has raised receptivity, but how do you really know whether the customer is ready to work with you in exploring her needs?

   You don't, unless you ask. So, right after explaining your purpose and the tentative benefit, probe her receptivity. An open-end probe will usually do the job ("How does that sound?"). If you get a positive answer, go on to the next component. If the answer is negative ("I don't really think I'm interested"), probe to find out why, then try to raise receptivity before going on. As you now know, there's no point in going forward to exploring her needs unless the customer's willing to go with you.

Explore the Customer's Needs

Q4 exploration of needs tries to:

1. *Confirm (or disprove) your existing idea.* These are the assumptions you've made about the customer's tangible and intangible needs prior to the sales call.
2. *Uncover new tangible and intangible needs.* These are unanticipated needs you know nothing about or may not even suspect.
3. *Create needs.* As you explore needs, make the customer aware of your products, services, and capabilities, and then determine whether the customer is interested. In essence, you are creating needs. You must, however, be disciplined so that you educate and create but avoid making a product and service presentation until the customer has prioritized her needs.

4. *Get the customer to acknowledge and prioritize her needs.* Say out loud that they exist, that you're aware of them, and which needs are most important to her.
5. *Establish your expertise.* Prove, by skillful, intelligent probing, that you know what you're doing.

The whole purpose of this second component is to furnish you with the information and the credibility you'll need to develop benefit statements that will pay off.

Here's how a Q4 exploration of needs is conducted:

1. *Probe the customer's tangible and intangible needs.* Remember, customers don't often express outright their intangible needs. Six probes are especially useful for finding out both kinds:
   - **Open-end probes.** Ideal for getting the customer to talk about her needs ("What are you presently doing to provide retirement benefits for your administrative people?").
   - **Pauses.** If the customer uses Q2 behavior, you'll probably have to use several open-end probes, each followed by a pause. Remember to hold the pause until the customer says something.
   - **Neutral probes.** Once the customer gets started, keep her going with neutral probes so you get full insight into her needs ("Fill me in on your profit-sharing feature.").
   - **Reflective statements.** If the discussion gets sticky, clear the air with reflective statements ("You're obviously not very happy with the treatment you got.").
   - **Summary statements.** Whatever the customer tells you, summarize it from time to time to make certain you've got it right ("As I understand it . . . .").
   - **Closed-end questions.** You'll need some closed-end questions to pin down details. Use them sparingly, or you may choke off discussion ("How many years of employment are needed to get full-vested rights?").

2. *Summarize the customer's needs.* When you think you've learned all that's necessary, sum up your understanding of the customer's needs, and ask him to confirm or reject your summary.
3. *Probe the customer's receptivity before going on.* At this point, you're almost ready for the "heart" of the presentation, in which you prove that your product or service solution will satisfy the customer's needs and deliver net gain. The crucial question is: Is the customer ready? Will he listen with an open mind? If not, you're in for some rough sailing. So, before setting out, use an open-end probe to determine whether the customer's ready for your product or service presentation. For example:

   "Fine. Now, how do you feel about taking a look at our senior-years program to see how you can overcome the defects in your present program at no extra cost?"

   The phrasing of the open-end question is important. If you can, weave in a benefit statement ("You can overcome the drawbacks in your present program at no extra cost."). This way, you remind the customer that he stands to gain something by listening to your presentation.

Present Your Product or Service

This is the "proof" stage of your call, when you demonstrate that your product or service solution will fill the customer's needs and, thus, deliver a net gain. Every Q4 presentation tries to:

1. *Generate understanding.* Get the customer to see how and why your product or service solution will fill her needs.
2. *Generate tentative commitment.* Get the customer thinking, "Because this product will fill my need, maybe I should buy it."

Don't expect much more than tentative commitment at this point. Although the customer thinks she may buy, she's probably also thinking of reasons she shouldn't. This is only normal.

Here's how a Q4 presentation is conducted:

1. *Deliver a benefit statement.* We saw how this is done in Chapter 5. To recap: Restate the customer's need, prove that your product

or service can fill it, and personalize the benefit by focusing on this particular customer. If the proof is long or complicated, space it out. Follow the guidelines in Chapters 8 and 9 for building trust, understanding, and commitment.

2. *Probe for the customer's acceptance.* Don't move to the next benefit until she understands and accepts the first one. Try an open-end probe ("How does that strike you?" or "What's your reaction?"). If her answer shows she doesn't understand or hasn't accepted what you've said, go back and straighten things out.
3. *Check the customer's receptivity.* Likewise, before going on to the next benefit, make certain the customer is ready: "Can we move on to the cash-reserve feature and see how it'll cut your costs?" If she's reluctant, probe to find out why, and straighten it out.
4. *Deliver another benefit statement.* Once the customer is ready for the next benefit, repeat the cycle. Continue until you've completely proven all the benefits your product or service can deliver. Don't waste time on information that has nothing to do with her needs. Make your benefit statements about real benefits, ways the product or service will pay off for this customer.
5. *Summarize the benefits, and check for omissions.* Once you've told the whole story, summarize the benefits ("Okay, let me recap what this plan will do for you . . . ."). Then, check to see if you've omitted anything the customer wants to know.
6. *Prove net gain.* Now that you've told the benefit story, you still have to prove net gain. Knowing the benefits of your product and service solution is the understanding part of the process. Although your customer may understand you perfectly, her commitment may still be weak or non-existent. She may be thinking, "Sounds like a good deal, but not nearly as good as what I can get from company X," or, "That's an impressive list of benefits, but it still doesn't add up to what I've already got."

   Now is the time to do some comparison selling. Stack up your benefits against those she's considering from other sources. Show that your total package of benefits will deliver more satisfaction — more need fulfillment — than any other package.

7. *Check receptivity.* Once you know you haven't overlooked any of the customer's needs, check to see if she's ready to move into our next stage of the call, managing objections ("Can I get your reaction to all this?" or "What's your evaluation of the plan I've laid out?").

   Don't assume that she is happy with your presentation, having completed all the components to this point. Let her speak her mind, even if you don't like what you hear. If you're going to close the call with understanding and commitment, you must first let the customer voice her objections and get them cleared up. That's what managing objections is all about.

Manage Objections

Objections can come up at any time, but they are most likely to take place right after you've presented your product or service. If the customer doesn't bring them up on her own, now is the time to probe for them. If you take for granted that silence means agreement, you may be in for a shock when you try to close and the customer refuses to buy. Immediately after your presentation is the logical time to deal with objections, but the techniques can be applied any time an objection comes up.

Q4 management of objections does three things:

1. *Shows you're willing to face up to objections.* This is important. It bolsters your standing with the customer to say, in effect, "I'm confident of my product and my ability to explain it and have nothing to hide."
2. *Uncovers the real objection.* Many stated objections cover up real objections the customer would rather not talk about. Only the real objection is worth managing.
3. *Generates commitment.* Objections either prevent or dilute commitment. An objection means "I'm not fully convinced." The only way to get full commitment is to get rid of the objection.

When is the best time to answer an objection? We said it can occur anytime. Should it be answered as soon as it occurs? That depends on two factors:

1. *The timing of the objection.* If an objection comes early in the presentation, your effective answer to it may depend on information the customer doesn't have yet. Technical questions in particular are often only answerable after certain facts and groundwork have been established. When a customer jumps the gun this way, you will probably want to defer answering.

   For example:

   Customer: Your ads say the Model 720 uses computer chips that don't contain silicon. I've been in electrical engineering for 20 years, and that doesn't sound right. I think your company is making claims that just defy logic.

   Salesperson: I can appreciate your being skeptical. It's a new technology. But once I've explained our new system for printing circuits, I think you'll see why we don't need silicon. But let me address what you're saying a little later, okay?

   Customer: Of course. I wasn't trying to rush you.

2. *The customer's receptivity.* If a customer is so engrossed in an objection that it keeps him from concentrating on anything else, you have no choice but to deal with it at that moment. If you put him off, his receptivity to anything else you say may plunge while he anticipates discussing the objection. If he brings up the objection a second or third time, clear it away before you proceed.

Another important point about objections is that there are two types, objective and subjective. Objective objections are objections that are real. They are genuine and exist in real time and space. Concerns about cost, delivery, availability, credit, service, warranties, etc., are objective. When your customer makes an objective objection ("Your price is too high."), he probably means it, although he could be covering up an objection he prefers to keep to himself ("I don't trust your company to be fair with me.").

Subjective objections are about the customer's feelings — his intangible needs, emotions, frame of mind, personal relationships.

"I don't know why, but I just don't like the idea," or "I've got a brother-in-law in the business, and I really ought to buy from him," are examples that contrast with objective objections.

Subjective objections may be real or fabricated. A customer who says, "I'm just not certain," may mean it, but he may also be covering up another objection that he hesitates to reveal to you.

So, before you can manage an objection, you must determine what the real objection is. To do so, we advocate a four-step procedure called APAC. APAC is an acronym for **A**cknowledge, **P**robe, **A**nswer, and **C**onfirm. Here's how it works:

1. *Acknowledge the objective objection voiced by the customer.* You shouldn't avoid answering it. It's not a threat. It's a chance to give more information or clear up what he doesn't understand. Show that you take it seriously. Think of an objection as a request for more information.

   Don't interpret the objection at this point or reword it to make it say what you think the customer means. Simply restate the objection in a summary statement as you heard it ("Paul, as I understand it, you think our first-year cost will run higher than your own in-company plan.").
2. *Probe until you fully understand the objection.* If it's an objective objection, it will usually deal with outside factors, such as cost, delivery, availability, etc. If it's a subjective objection that's not genuine, your probing should uncover the real objection.
3. *Answer the objection.* If you can, answer it by developing a proof statement. Don't rely on claims and vague assurances. Cite evidence. If possible, convert your answer to a benefit statement that not only removes the objection, but also adds to your presentation strength.
4. *Confirm his understanding of your answer.* Never assume that because you've answered the objection to your satisfaction, you've answered it to the customer's satisfaction. Instead, use an open- or closed-end question to see if he's satisfied ("How do you feel about the warranty now?" or "Does that set your mind to rest?"). If he's not satisfied, go back over your answer.

The procedure changes somewhat for managing subjective objections. Here's why:

- *It's not easy to tell if subjective objections are real or made up.* You'll have to do some careful probing. It won't be easy, because when the objection is phony, the customer is obviously reluctant to talk about the real reason.
- *If the objection is made up, it could be masking a worse subjective objection.* The statement, "I'll have to talk to my partner," may be a customer's way of using Q2 or Q3 behavior to conceal an accusatory objection, such as, "I don't think I can rely on your word." Or, it may conceal an objective objection, "Your price is too high." Either way, probing won't be easy.
- *Your first challenge, then, is to find out if the subjective objection is real or phony.* When it's phony, you have to identify the real objection. Either way, your goal is to find out what's actually bothering the customer.

Figure 21 shows how to use APAC to manage objections.

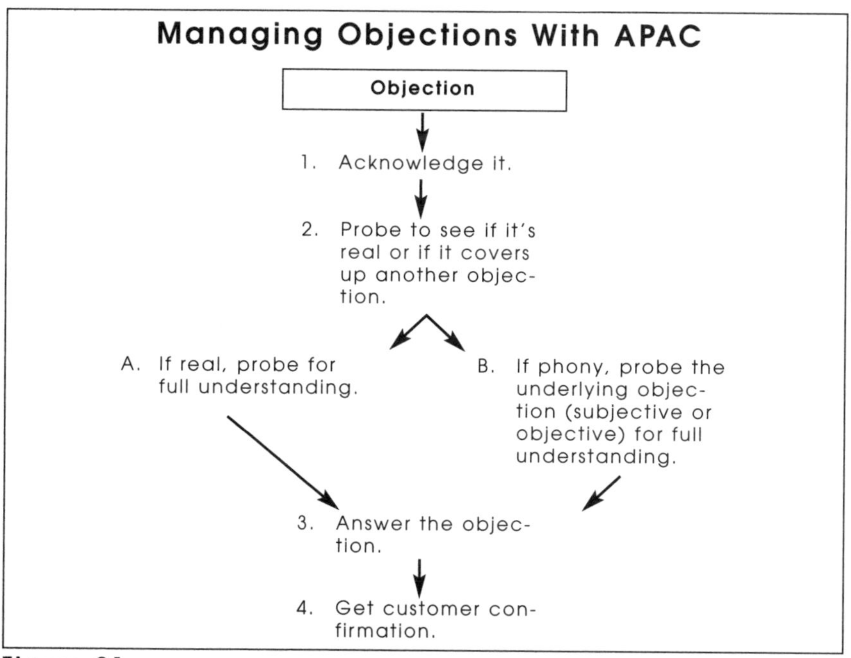

Figure 21

An example in which the subjective objection covers up an objective one follows:

Customer: Sounds good, Al. But I can't do a thing today. Gotta talk to Roy first.

Salesperson: Fine, Max. Why not bring him in right now?

Customer: No way. He's out of town. Extended buying trip. Won't get back for a couple of weeks.

Salesperson: I see. Well, can we set up a meeting for the three of us when he gets back?

Customer: No. That's not necessary. I can talk to him alone.

Salesperson: Well, if you're going to do that, let me make certain you've got all the information you'll need. What have I failed to make clear?

Customer: Nothing. Nothing at all. I understand it perfectly.

Salesperson: Good. Then what concerns do you have? What doubts?

Customer: (A bit hesitant) No doubts. No serious doubts anyway.

Salesperson: No serious doubts. How about minor doubts?

Customer: Aw, just one. No big deal.

Salesperson: I'm glad to hear that, Max. However, if you've got any doubts, it's my job to try and clear them up. What's the one doubt that's bothering you?

Customer: It's not exactly bothering me, Al. I really don't want to make a big thing out of it.

Salesperson: Keep going.

Customer: Look, I don't want you to take this personally.

Salesperson: Believe me, Max, I won't. Our relationship's strong enough to stand some straight talk. Go ahead.

Customer: Well, it's that letter.

Salesperson: What letter?

Customer: The one from your credit department. About three months ago. That really hurt.

Salesperson: What do you mean?

Customer: Well, I explained to your credit manager that I was having some collection problems of my own and that I'd pay the invoice as soon as I could. It seemed to me they should've been willing to trust an old customer. When I got that letter, well, it was like being hit in the face with cold water. A real shock.

Salesperson: Go on.

Customer: Collection agency! Imagine, threatening to turn my account over to a collection agency. Al, nothing like that's happened to me in 22 years of business. Now, mind you, I'm not blaming you.

Salesperson: I understand that. Perfectly. It must've been plenty upsetting. Let me ask you a few questions . . . .

This illustrates the subjective objection ("Gotta talk to Roy first.") disguising an objective objection ("Your credit company's credit policies are brutal."). This happens frequently with customers with strong Q2 or Q3 tendencies.

Another example, in which the subjective objection is real, follows.

Customer: Okay, I've got the picture. Why don't you leave your catalog and a price list? I'll get back to you.

Salesperson: Any questions you'd like to get cleared up first?

Customer: No, I don't think so.

Salesperson: Well, then, wouldn't it be to your advantage to place the order today so you can get delivery faster?

Customer: No, I want to think about it.

Salesperson: You're uncertain.

Customer: Yeah, I guess I am. It sounds good, but I just don't know.

Salesperson: What exactly are you uncertain about?

Customer: I'm just not certain it's a better deal than what I'm getting now. I can't point to any flaws in your proposal. I just don't feel confident enough to go ahead with it.

Salesperson: You think you might be better off sticking with what you've got.

Customer: That's just it. I'm not certain. I wish I was, but I'm not.

Salesperson: Okay, then, maybe it'll help if we go over this comparative two-year cost projection . . . .

In many cases, no matter how they're worded, subjective objections boil down to one point: "I'm just not confident enough to buy now." The customer is not convinced of the net gain. He hasn't been persuaded to act.

Close the Sales Call

Every Q4 close tries to do two things:

1. *Confirm the customer's understanding.* Get the customer to acknowledge that she's clear on what the call was all about.
2. *Confirm the customer's commitment.* Get the customer to take whatever action the call was intended to stimulate.

The bottom line is that a successful close is any conclusion to a sales call that does what the call was intended to do — advance a sale. Yet, it's one of the saddest sights in selling to see a salesperson who works hard and effectively until the close and, then, sabotages his own efforts by saying something like, "I'll leave our brochure and get back to you in a few weeks," or "I'm certain you'll want time to think about it; give me a call when you decide," or "That's my story; when you're ready to do something, let me know."

Why would an otherwise competent salesperson back away from the whole point of a sales presentation — closing the sale? There are three likely reasons:

1. *The close requires more assertiveness than any other part of the call.* Many salespeople equate assertiveness with being pushy or using high-pressure tactics. They consider any closing as a Q1 tactic and shy away from it.
2. *Many salespeople see the close as a threat to their self-esteem.* They are afraid of being turned down or put off. They take being turned down as a personal rejection.
3. *Many salespeople don't know how to close.* They're assertive enough and don't fear rejection, but they don't have the necessary skills to close effectively. Because they feel inept at this point, they sidestep the close.

If these Q2 or Q3 approaches to closing are self-defeating, the Q1 approach can fail also, although it aggressively tries to make a sale happen, as the next example shows:

Salesperson: Well, what do you think?

Customer: I'm just not convinced.

Salesperson: Come on! Why waste this opportunity? Just say the word, and I'll call the factory and tell them to load that truck. We can have it rolling this afternoon.

Customer: I don't know . . .

Salesperson: Listen, while we stand here talking, the price could go up. Believe me, you've got nothing to worry about. Just give me your signature, and I'll pick up that phone and call our plant manager.

Customer: I've got to have time to think.

Salesperson: There's nothing to think about. Take my word for it.

Q1 pressure sometimes works. Some customers do cave in and buy. But in a large number of cases, this Q1 squeeze only antagonizes the customer, drives down receptivity, and fumbles away a potential sale. What remains is the Q4 close.

Here's how the Q4 close is conducted:

1. *Summarize the benefits and the net gain.* Although the customer should know them by now, it's best to repeat the benefits and

the net gain. If you can, have the customer spell it out with a simple open-end probe ("Janet, before we wrap this up, let me ask you, what do you see in all this as the real payoff for you and your company?"). If you can't get the customer to do this, do it yourself.

2. *Ask for a commitment.* Remember, don't use Q2 or Q3 behavior at this point. Use Q4 assertiveness, and let the customer know you want the order by asking for it. There are two ways to do this: forced choice or by direct request.

   You can't use the forced-choice close technique when there is only one version of your product or service. But if there is a choice of model, style, color, size, or whatever, this technique can be very useful ("Which plan meets your needs best, the quarterly payment with straight interest or the annual payment with compound interest?").

   This method doesn't make the customer feel pushed, which is especially helpful for keeping a customer who has been using Q2 or Q3 behavior from feeling pressured.

   The direct-request close consists of a summary statement followed by a probe, usually a close-end question, such as: "Donna, you've said you must bring down costs by year's end. I've shown that our product can help you do that *(benefit and net gain statement)*. Shall we go ahead and install our system?"

   This is the epitome of Q4 assertiveness. It asks for the order in the most direct way, but it still avoids Q1 hostile aggressiveness.

3. *Manage the customer's response.* You'll get one of four responses:

   - A firm yes. Confirm it and move on to the action plan.
   - A qualified yes. It's usually a "Yes, but . . . ." statement, such as, "Yes, but before you write up the order . . . ." or "Yes, but I'm still not certain about one thing . . . ." A qualified yes normally either asks for more information or offers a minor objection. Summarize the qualification, ask the customer to confirm the summary, handle the problem, and then ask for a commitment again.

- An objection. This indicates you still haven't resolved the customer's doubts ("I don't know; I'm still bothered by that tax liability."). Go back to managing objections.
- A flat no. Probe the reasons, and handle them. Don't give up without a try. A surprisingly large number of flat nos aren't really as flat as they sound. The reasons for saying no may be objections that you can respond to and, perhaps, that open the door to discussion. If you can eliminate the objections, it may prove that the flat rejection wasn't as firm as it sounded.

In some cases, although the customer has said no, he may expect you to dig in and try to change his mind. He may respect tenacity and persistence on your part, feeling it is part of your job to persuade him to your view. So, although you should show respect for a "no" answer, it doesn't necessarily mean the sale is over. Most people like dealing with Q4 assertiveness. It's worth a try to test a flat no.

4. *Work out an action plan and conclude the call.* Once you have the customer's commitment, determine his decision-making process and work out the details of quantity, date of delivery, terms, etc. Then, pave the way for the next call ("I'll phone next week to set up a follow-up appointment. That way, we can iron out any installation problems right away."). Thank the customer, and move on to your next call.

Service After the Sale

Signing the order is really just the beginning of a business relationship for buyers and sellers.

Today's sophisticated customers expect their salesperson to act as a "go to" person and a problem solver. Meeting those expectations maintains customer satisfaction after the sale and helps build stable relationships. Recent research indicates that it requires seven calls to sell a new customer, and three to sell a satisfied existing customer. These findings substantiate the importance of service after the sale.

The Q4 salesperson confirms the customer's expectations and works to accomplish a smooth implementation of products and services. Q4 salespeople make it a point to personally monitor customer satisfaction with frequent follow-up probes, such as, "How are we doing?" or "What would you like to see improved?" In addition, they may use formal satisfaction surveys.

In Q4 selling, follow-up or service calls not only present opportunities to increase business, but to improve performance. The salesperson reads, searches the buyer's web site, and asks questions to stay current and informed: "What's going on that I should be aware of?" "I read about some expansion plans on your company web site; how will these plans affect you?" These types of questions promote sales and build relationships.

By maintaining contact and monitoring customer satisfaction, Q4 salespeople discover valuable problem-solving opportunities that help solidify their relationships with customers. After establishing a successful track record for service after the sale, they are in a favorable position to ask for referrals, which provide new possibilities for networking inside and outside of the buyer's organization.

With Q4 selling skills, a salesperson can ensure customer satisfaction, building business relationships that ward off competition.

Other Considerations

The Trial Close

Whether it's called a "trial close," "attempt to close," "closing effort," or some other name, this is sometimes characterized as a special sales presentation tactic to find out if a customer is ready to buy. Strictly speaking, however, every attempt to close is a trial close. You are testing out the customer's intentions. As such, it is an effective tactic only if it's done at the right time and in the right way.

The Right Time

Some trial closes take place exactly when they should in the sequence we have laid out. However, many are premature. They come far too early in the presentation, before receptivity has been raised, before needs have been explored, before benefits have been proven, and before objections have been managed. So, they are usually a waste of time.

In fact, Q1 trial closes are even worse. They may push a customer from feeling neutral about the sale to actively resisting it. This makes the salesperson's job that much harder. He now has to turn the customer completely around.

A timely trial close virtually always occurs after the other components of the presentation, but does it have to? Not if the customer initiates the close before then. If, in the middle of stating benefits, the customer breaks in and says he is ready to buy, then, by all means, close the sale right away.

Most customers wait for the salesperson to initiate the close. The distinction here is between a trial close and the actual close. A trial close is an attempt to discover if the customer is ready to buy, and normally occurs only after you have explored needs, made your presentation, and managed objections. Attempting it any sooner would be premature. If the trial close verifies the customer's desire to buy, it's time to move on to the actual close.

The Right Way

As with all stages of a sale, a trial close can be done in a Q1, Q2, Q3, or Q4 manner.

A Q1 trial close is high-pressure and coercive ("What are you waiting for? Do you want to be the only person in the industry who missed out on this offer?").

A Q2 trial close is weak and pessimistic ("I guess you've already got all the inventory you need, huh?").

A Q3 trial close is offhanded, personalized ("You know, I'd never in a million years put pressure on you. Whatever you decide is your business, and I'll understand perfectly. Do what you think is best. I value our friendship too much to feel otherwise.").

A Q4 trial close comes at the right time, keeps receptivity high, is assertive but not domineering, and is businesslike, not personal. It has the best chance of being effective.

Not All Closes Produce a Sale

Many calls aren't intended to produce sales at that particular time. They're made to achieve goals that will lead to sales on later calls. So, in considering the close, keep three things in mind:

1. *Every Q4 call has a specific purpose.* It may be to set up a presentation, to handle a complaint, follow up a sale, and so forth. But there is no such thing as a pointless Q4 call.
2. *Whatever the purpose, the call should end with a close.* That is, you should "nail down" whatever you came to accomplish by making certain the customer understands, is committed, and is willing to proceed.
3. *The closing techniques we've described can be used to close any call, no matter what the purpose.*

Format Modifications

All Q4 calls follow the Structured Sales Call Format, but some elements within the format may be emphasized more on some calls than on others.

On a fact-finding call, for instance, *exploring customer's needs* will be emphasized. *Presenting the product or service* will probably shrink to a mere statement of future action ("I'll be back Tuesday morning with a proposal."), and *managing objections* may shrink to almost nothing. The salesperson will at least give the customer a chance to voice objections ("Can you see any flaws in the way we're operating so far?"). In Q4 selling, each of the five components is at least initiated, although, in some cases, it may not be developed.

What's Next?

After learning how to structure a sales call, what is left to know about Q4 relationship selling? Although this format gives you the procedures, strategies, and tactics for developing the sale, it doesn't explain how you should deal with the unique characteristics of the customers you meet. Is there a strategy for handling belligerent Q1 customer behavior? Q2 behavior? Q3 behavior? The next chapter will show how your Q4 approach can be tailored to deal with anyone.

CHAPTER 11

The Q4 Strategies

What's the most important ingredient in selling your particular product or service? Price? Quality? Unique features?

Any of these could be the net gain your customers will receive doing business with you. More than likely, a combination of benefits are important to them. But what if your price is better than your competitor's, but your delivery time is slower? Or suppose your product is superior, but your price is not as attractive?

It's often difficult for customers to weigh benefits against one another. Customers don't always make their purchasing decisions based on objective comparisons. It turns out, then, that the ultimate net gain, the factor that tips the scales in your favor, is often you. As we've said, all else being equal, customers are likely to buy from the salesperson most responsive to their needs. Is that how you are perceived?

One advantage you have in applying your Q4 relationship selling skills is that you can help yourself become the ultimate net gain by applying them in a strategic way.

What Is a Q4 Strategy?

A Q4 strategy is an overall plan for achieving the objectives of a particular sales call. The Q4 skills are your tactics to be used at specific points to persuade during the call. You weave them together into an overall pattern designed specifically for the customer with whom you're dealing.

Thus, no two Q4 strategies are identical. Although there are basic Q4 strategies for Q1, Q2, Q3, or Q4 customer behavior, each is modified on different calls. Even if you make five straight calls on customers who use Q1 behavior, and you use the Q4 strategy for Q1 customer behavior, you'll still have to modify it to the individual needs of your customer. Your ability to devise and carry out a Q4 strategy is what enables you to become the net gain — the factor that convinces the customer to feel, "I'll be better off buying from this salesperson than from anyone else."

To clarify this, let's look again at the three pathways to a sale.

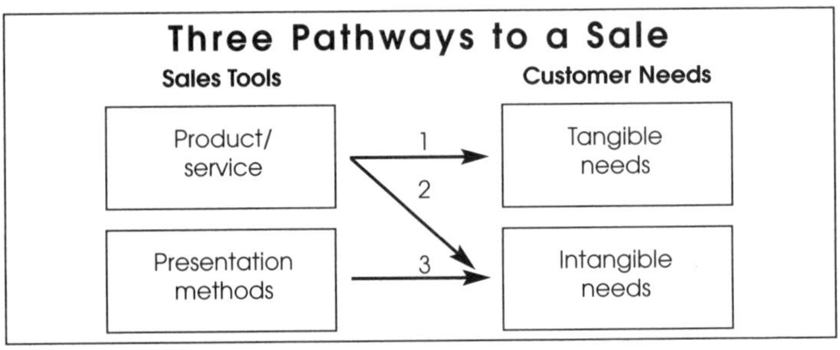

As the diagram shows, your customer's tangible needs can be filled by your product or service (pathway 1), and the intangible needs can be filled by both your product or service (pathway 2) and by your presentation methods (pathway 3).

The Road to Pathway 3

As we said, it's possible to fill a customer's intangible needs by your product or service (pathway 2). However, your competitor's products or services may also fill those needs or possibly even do a better job. You can't really do much to affect the price of your product. You can't control how long it takes for it to be shipped. You can't control some bad publicity your product may have received.

In other words, what happens in pathways 1 and 2 may be largely determined by your home office, the factory, the credit department, the billing department, and so on.

You can't do much to change the situation. However, as we pointed out in Chapter 4, pathway 3 is special. It's the only one completely under your control. You can affect how you sell.

Remember, whether or not you increase receptivity, how thoroughly you probe, whether or not you uncover the customer's needs before presenting benefits, the way you handle objections, that is, the skill with which you tailor your presentation to this customer, is up to you. This chapter explains how to make pathway 3 work for you by tailoring your presentation methods in a Q4 manner to respond to the intangible needs of this particular customer.

The Q4 Strategies: An Overview

Figure 22 (pages 146 and 147) deserves careful reading. It will acquaint you with each strategy and let you compare them. Note that all the strategies stick to the Structured Sales Call Format, and each strategy follows its own general guidelines.

The Q4 Strategy for Q1 Customer Behavior

Q1 behavior is generally motivated by strong needs for esteem and independence. To deal with them, keep these guidelines in mind:

1. *Stress benefits that provide status, importance, prestige, autonomy, control, and freedom of action.* This is fundamental. This customer wants to look good, make an impression, and be his own person. If you can, make it plain that your product or service can gratify these needs. More than that, gratify them yourself during the sales call.

   Above all, be respectful. Listen with interest to his views and opinions. Seek his advice. Let him boast. If he says something that impresses you, say so. If necessary, bring in high-status

Q4 Strategies for the Structured Sales Call Format

Phases of the Sale	Q1 Customer Behavior	Q2 Customer Behavior	Q3 Customer Behavior	Q4 Customer Behavior
Open the call	• Set a brisk but cordial tone; hold down small talk • Aim benefits at esteem and independence needs • Expect open resistance	• Set a friendly, relaxed tone, but don't use Q3 behavior • Aim benefits at security needs • Expect silence, indifference	• Set an amiable tone, but don't use Q3 behavior • Aim benefits at social needs • Expect meandering and easy yeses	• Set a businesslike, helpful tone • Aim benefits at needs for new and better • Expect high receptivity
Explore customer needs	• Expect negative flat assertions • Vent negative emotions (put-downs, belligerence) • Use open-end probes; listen carefully; summarize • Perform process checks	• Expect short, unhelpful answers • Vent negative emotions (tension, reluctance) • Listen patiently; use pauses • Use many open-end probes • Perform process checks	• Expect rambling, positive answers • Vent positive emotions (optimism, exuberance) • Control rambling with closed-end probes • Perform process checks	• Expect helpful, relevant answers • Use the full range of probes, especially open-end probes, neutral probes, summary statements, reflective statements
Present product or service	• Voice strong convictions; don't make flat assertions • Stress esteem and independence benefits • Support proof with plenty of organized data; get feedback	• Moderate your pace; pause frequently • Stress security benefits • Be factual, but don't machine-gun facts; invite frequent feedback	• Relax the pace; allow occasional meandering • Stress social benefits • Don't overburden with details • Probe easy yeses	• Voice strong convictions; don't make flat assertions • Stress new and better benefits • Be factual; invite feedback

Manage objections	• Encourage customer to sum up objections • Vent resistance with reflective statements; don't use leading questions • Don't expect full agreement	• Probe carefully; don't assume silence means approval • Go easy on closed-end and leading questions • Don't expect much enthusiasm	• Probe carefully; easy yeses may hide strong objections • Go easy on open-end probes and pauses • Don't expect full candor	• Ask customer to sum up objections • Rely mainly on open-end probes and summary statements • Expect candor; and if you handle the objection well, agreement
Close the call	• Encourage the customer to sum up benefits • Expect a qualified yes, an objection, or a flat no • Let the customer take the lead in working out action plan	• Be prepared to sum up benefits yourself • Expect a qualified yes or an objection • Lead the customer in working out an action plan	• Take the lead in summarizing benefits • Expect a firm yes, a qualified yes, or an objection • Lead the customer in working out an action plan	• Encourage the customer to sum up benefits • Expect a firm yes or no backed up by solid reasons • Jointly work out an action plan

Figure 22

people from your own company to meet with him. Don't be too familiar or informal, unless you know the customer well and are very certain of what you're doing.

2. *Expect anger, belligerence, sarcasm, put-downs, deep-seated skepticism, objection-hopping, flat assertions, impatience, dogmatism.* This is what Q1 behavior is all about. It's the customer's way of saying, "I don't need you" (independence need) or "I'm smarter than you" (esteem need). If you understand Q1 behavior, none of this should surprise you. Anticipate it.

3. *Address and vent Q1 anger and probe flat assertions.* To handle the anger, use reflective statements such as, "You're really concerned," "I can tell you're bothered," or "You don't sound happy with it." If you haven't had much experience using reflective statements, you may feel awkward at first. But you'll soon feel comfortable with them, and they are indispensable in Q1 situations.

   Don't ignore flat assertions. Many contain a nugget of truth, and that nugget could be very important. So, probe until you strip away the exaggeration and find out what's really bothering this customer.

4. *Stay cool and don't let the customer think he's getting to you.* This is vital. If he gets the idea he's got you off-balance, he may push his advantage. That will probably upset you even more. Once you paint yourself into this corner, you may have real trouble getting out. So, try not to get rattled in the first place. Or, if you do, don't let it show. You should be able to manage it if you approach the call realistically, that is, you expect to get a "hard time."

5. *Show conviction and strength without sounding cocky, argumentative, or aggressive.* Because this customer admires strength, it's good to convince him that you know and believe in whatever you're saying. So, present your proof of benefits with vigor, assurance, and conviction. However, avoid making flat assertions ("This is the greatest product ever developed."). This will only arouse disbelief and the feeling you are trying to fool him.

6. *Don't argue.* Probe first, and, then, reason. If the customer contradicts you, offers an objection, or tries to pick a fight, do two things: Probe first to raise receptivity, and find out what the resistance is all about. Then, use reason. Use data and logic to make your point. If you probe skillfully enough, you may get the customer to make your point for you. This will strengthen your case while bolstering his self-esteem.

   Whatever happens, don't argue. With his strong needs for esteem and independence, this customer isn't about to let you win, and you can't change that. You can accomplish so much more by probing and reasoning.

7. *Make certain the customer doesn't lose face.* This is implicit in everything we've said. What might cause this customer to lose face, to feel embarrassed? Going over his head without first telling him, making calls without first seeking an appointment, depreciating her achievements, failing to keep your word or an appointment, and so on. The thing to guard against is the unintentional insult. Very few salespeople deliberately inflame customers, but many do so unwittingly. Be careful with this customer. A heedless slip could be disastrous.

8. *Let the customer take credit for good ideas — even if they're yours.* After all, you don't really care who gets credit for an idea, as long as you get credit for the sale. So, if the customer appropriates one of your suggestions, fine. If he insists he said something that you know full well you actually said, let it go. And by all means, if he does come up with an idea that's useful, clever, or innovative, give him full credit. Never hesitate to pay this customer a deserved compliment.

9. *Rely mainly on open-end probes and summary and reflective statements.* Use few or no leading questions. The value of open-end probes is that they tell the customer, "I really do want to hear your views." The value of summary and reflective statements is that they tell the customer, "I've been paying close attention. I understand what you're saying." They make him feel respected and independent. The danger of leading questions is that

they tell the customer, "I have no qualms about putting words in your mouth." They make him feel diminished and dependent. So, use them sparingly and cautiously.

10. *Be ready to shift your strategy if the customer's behavior shifts.* Once you've sized up the customer's behavior as Q1, don't get locked into your diagnosis. Be alert to changes in the behavior, and modify or change your strategy accordingly. After all, people are changeable. If his behavior changes while yours stays in a rut, you may lose control of the call. Stay flexible.

The Q4 Strategy for Q2 Customer Behavior

Q2 behavior is motivated mostly by strong needs for security. To deal with them, keep these guidelines in mind:

1. *Stress benefits that provide stability, low risk, assured outcome, proven value, permanence, durability.* Tie your proof statements to the customer's desire for assurance ("This program's been used successfully for 20 years.") and stability ("Our company's been making these units longer than anyone in the field."). This customer doesn't want to be a trailblazer or pioneer. So, don't stress new or innovative features. Instead, convey a sense of reliability. Sound confident, but not bombastic; knowledgeable, but not pretentious; friendly, but not too familiar; and helpful, but not over-solicitous. Keep it low-key.

   In describing benefits, use any sales aids that will reassure the customer: testimonials, references, case studies, independent laboratory reports, surveys, and so on. Let the customer know that your proposal isn't new or untried. Show her it's worked before for other people.

2. *Expect the customer to be remote, uncommunicative, hard to read, distrustful, and apprehensive.* You'll find it much easier to be patient and persistent if you anticipate the problems we've described. If you've talked with the customer before and her earlier behavior has been mostly Q2, it's reasonable to assume it'll be that way again. So, go into the call telling yourself, "This will be a challenge. This customer will probably keep her dis-

tance and make me work for every scrap of information I get. But I better suppress any annoyance and not push. I don't want to give her the idea I'm pressuring her."

3. *Address Q2 silence, withdrawal, or skepticism.* Unlike the obvious causes of Q1 anger, the causes of Q2 doubt and skepticism may not be readily apparent. Silence, for example, may not mean agreement. Q2 behavior cues demand observation, identification, and immediate action. A nod of disapproval or frown can be effectively addressed with a reflective statement such as, "Alice, you appear to have some doubts about the service." Then, pause, listen to Alice's reply, and respond accordingly.

4. *Be patient.* Don't rush yourself or the customer. Don't pressure. The tempo of the presentation is crucial. If you move too fast or throw too much at the customer, she'll feel pressured, and her initial distrust will intensify. Lower your voice, and slow down your delivery. Pause often to let her absorb your ideas, and check periodically for her reaction.

   Remember that this customer probably has a stereotype of salespeople as high-pressure pitchmen. If you appear to be pushy, you'll only confirm the stereotype.

5. *Show genuine concern.* Let the customer know you're not there just to advance your own interests. The problem is that because this customer doesn't talk much about her concerns, it's hard for you to know what they are. To find out, you must get him to open up. That requires patient, persistent probing. If you don't probe tenaciously and give her plenty of time to respond, you're not likely to learn much and won't be able to show your own concern. You'll have to control your frustration and stay cool no matter how tightlipped and uncooperative the customer may be.

6. *Establish trust, using the trust-building guidelines we've described.* All the guidelines we developed in Chapter 8 will help. The one that may help the most, although it will be the most difficult, is to maintain two-way involvement. Q2 behavior resists

involvement; but if you don't draw the customer into the presentation and make her a participant in the discussion, you probably won't build much trust and won't have much chance of making the sale.

To maintain two-way involvement, probe persistently and listen patiently. This won't be easy, because your impulse will be to stop probing and start telling the customer what her needs are. Resist this impulse, and keep probing without rushing the customer, putting words in her mouth, or finishing her sentences. Pause after each probe. That's the only way you can find out what her story is.

7. *Guide firmly but gently.* This customer won't take the initiative. So, you'll have to, but in a low-key way. Beneath most Q2 behavior is a desire for guidance. Ironically, although the customer is acting aloof or remote, she actually would prefer sharing the burden of making up her mind with someone else. It's just that she first must be convinced that you are knowledgeable, competent, and reliable. She needs to feel comfortable and secure in leaning on you. Once you establish trust, she'll feel secure in following your lead. Guide her without pushing. Get her to seek your advice, and then give it, showing unobtrusive strength.

8. *Let the customer keep his self-respect.* Don't mock or tease. It's easy to belittle Q2 behavior. The customer may strike you as meek and indecisive, but he certainly doesn't want to be told about it. Remarks such as, "What's the matter? Can't make up your mind?" will be taken as insults. If the customer thinks you're humiliating him, even if that's not your intention, he'll probably get back at you by refusing to buy.

   Paradoxically, customers who don't seem very strong can behave with remarkable strength when their pride is at stake. In the last analysis, a customer who uses Q2 behavior may be no more willing to lose face than a customer who uses Q1 behavior.

9. *Rely mainly on open-end probes, pauses, and brief assertions.* Go easy on leading and closed-end questions. As we've said, to get this customer to open up, you'll have to use open-end probes, followed by pauses to allow response time. Once she has opened up, use brief assertions and neutral probes to keep her talking. Because she'll probably convey information in small amounts, you'll probably have to use a lot of these probes.

   Go easy on closed-end and leading questions. After all, you can't get a customer to open up with closed-end probes, and you can't build trust with leading questions that will be taken as an attempt to back her into a corner.

10. *Be ready to shift your strategy if the customer's behavior changes.* Once this customer is convinced you can be trusted, she may surprise you. She may relax somewhat, talk more, and actually volunteer information. Be prepared to modify your strategy accordingly.

The Q4 Strategy for Q3 Customer Behavior

Q3 behavior is mostly motivated by strong social needs joined to fairly strong security and esteem needs. To deal with them, keep these guidelines in mind:

1. *Stress benefits that provide acceptance, popularity, and a chance to do something other people will appreciate.* This customer wants to be well liked — a thoughtful, considerate person who's accepted. Appeal to this interest by tying your proof statements to her social needs and, to a lesser extent, her security and esteem needs ("This system has proven popular everywhere it's been tried" or "This plan is a fine opportunity for you to boost the morale of your employees").

   More than that, be accepting. Personal relationships are critically important to this customer, so make a particular effort to build rapport.

2. *Expect the customer to be enthusiastic and very agreeable.* Enthusiasm and instant agreement are common Q3 behavior.

Aimless rambling conversations and easily spoken yeses often cover up serious doubts.

3. *Address Q3 enthusiasm and determine whether agreement is genuine.* The challenge when working with Q3 behavior is to substantiate that all the effusive enthusiasm and agreement is real. This customer can say, "Terrific," after every sentence you utter and yet not really accept a thing you've said. Automatic agreement may be disguising her real thoughts. She could be hiding the fact that she doesn't want to hurt your feelings or get into a contentious discussion by disagreeing with you.

   To find out what the customer really thinks, you will have to probe and suggest that she has doubts ("Mary, it's gratifying to hear so much enthusiasm. But usually when people hear this proposal for the first time, they've got some serious reservations. After all, it is a pretty unusual approach. How about you? What are your doubts?"). It may take several such probes before she admits she's not as enthusiastic as she sounds.

   If you don't test these agreeable responses, you may get a rude shock when you try to close. Instead of the easy close that would seem to follow naturally from all that agreement, you may hear any number of false objections that hide her real evaluation of your product or service. She may say the timing's not right, the new budget hasn't been set, etc. In that case, you'll have to probe for the hidden objection.

4. *Be outgoing and friendly, but don't get sucked into the Q3 whirlpool or the whole presentation may drown in a sea of irrelevance.* This can easily happen. In building rapport, you don't want to be lured into subjects that have nothing to do with why you're there.

   A Q3 interruption, like "My daughter just won a scholarship to MIT!" must be acknowledged with genuine interest. A reflective statement such as, "You must be pleased with her achievement," gives the customer permission to tell you about her child. After you have listened, this customer feels obligated and is more likely to be receptive to what you have to say.

With Q3 behavior, you may find it difficult to get back on track without hurting the customer's feelings. The best policy is not to get drawn in from the start.

This may not be easy. In fact, a certain amount of rambling may be unavoidable. This customer is hard to confine to one subject and sometimes hard to follow. Her easy approval ("Sounds great," "Terrific idea") may entice you into wandering away from your presentation. Deal with both by probing.

What if the conversation has derailed and is not getting anywhere? Time for a process check ("Jill, I get the feeling we're heading in four or five different directions, and we're going to find ourselves lost. What do you think we can do to get back on track?").

5. *Keep the focus on business, but loosen up enough to allow some meandering.* Control what's said, but not too tightly. If you do, you'll make the customer uneasy and distracted. If that happens, receptivity will plunge. So, you have to permit a bit of meandering here and there.

   The problem is this customer's long-winded, rambling conversation takes a lot of time without telling you very much. Once you've opened up the subject of needs, for example, you'll probably get a series of time-consuming responses but not much useful information. Moreover, the information is apt to be slanted, ignoring or downplaying any needs caused by you or your company. So you'll have to do some hard digging to get the whole story.

6. *Personalize the call.* Remember the customer's strong interest in people. You'll probably find that this customer is bored by abstractions, technical details, statistics, or anything impersonal. To capture and hold her attention, try to personalize and humanize the presentation. Talk about people's experiences with your product and their reactions to it. Mention names that you know are important to the customer.

While doing this, be careful not to downgrade anyone. This customer will be uncomfortable with negative talk about other people. If you can't say something positive or neutral about someone, don't mention him at all.

7. *Guide the customer firmly and make specific suggestions.* Like customers with strong Q2 needs, the typical customer with strong Q3 needs really does want guidance, but is more ready to trust you. This customer appreciates help with details. Because her own style is loose and disorganized, she'll look to you for structure and organization. Provide it not by telling her what to do, but by suggesting it ("Carla, it seems in view of everything we've talked about, you'll be better off with the model 270 instead of the 310.").

   As a rule, it's not a good idea during closing to give this customer options. A guided close, such as, "Jane, I think the lightweight model's best for you. Do you agree?" should prove more efficient than asking the customer to choose among three different options.

8. *Rely heavily on closed-end probes and summary and reflective statements.* Go easy on open-end probes and pauses. If you give this customer a chance to talk at length, she'll take it. So, control the opportunities and channel the talk (closed-end probes), isolate the essentials (summary statements), and vent those positive but interfering emotions (reflective statements).

9. *Be ready to shift your strategy if the customer's behavior changes.* There's no guarantee that nice, easygoing people will stay that way. Even Q3 behavior can change. If it does, be prepared to change with it.

The Q4 Strategy for Q4 Customer Behavior

Q4 behavior is generally motivated by strong self-realization and independence needs. To deal with them, keep these guidelines in mind:

1. *Stress benefits that provide something new, creative, innovative, pacesetting, experimental, or unusual.* This customer is receptive

to novelty but not for its own sake. If your proposal is really unique, he'll listen — if he thinks it might pay off. He's looking for better ways to achieve his goals. If he thinks he can find those better ways by buying something new or untried, he's much more likely to do it than those who practice Q1, Q2, or Q3 behavior. However, he won't buy if it seems rash or foolish. He takes calculated risks with the odds in his favor. It's up to you to prove they are.

2. *Expect the customer to be fully involved and give him every chance to be.* There's nothing withdrawn or passive about Q4 behavior. This customer will listen, but he'll also insist on speaking out. He'll ask questions, comment, or disagree. Encourage this. If you don't, you may stifle his need for independence and lower his receptivity.

3. *Be pragmatic.* Tie your product or service to the customer's goals or solutions, and prove that it will further his achievement. Because this customer must be convinced that he will benefit from it, his Q4 behavior is not easy to deal with. It's demanding and challenging. He wants hard proof of what's in it for him. He won't buy something just to please you or make you go away. He demands high competence on your part.

   We stress this point because many salespeople wrongly assume that Q4 customer behavior poses few or no problems. After all, how could anyone have trouble with customers who are reasonable, logical, and willing to listen? But those qualities are precisely why such customers can be very hard to deal with.

   "Reasonable" means making decisions on the basis of explanations and justifications. So, your claims can't be flimsy or unsupported generalities. They must be backed by solid reasons and explanations.

   "Logical" means basing decisions on systematic thinking. That means this customer won't have much patience with a disorganized or confused presentation.

"Willing to listen" means paying attention to something instructive and useful. This customer doesn't want to waste time. He expects to learn something worthwhile from the presentation.

This customer is not only tough, he's probing. He's very likely to ask you searching questions, to challenge you for documentation and comparisons, to prod you for details and insights.

What's the best way to deal with a Q4 customer? Pragmatically. Focus on results, the goals he hopes to achieve. Prove that with your product or service, he can reach those goals. The question he most wants answered is, "So what?" Always tie into his goals and give him practical reasons to buy. The next three guidelines follow from this one.

4. *Be direct and businesslike.* Assert authority, but don't make flat assertions. This customer admires strength. He'll respect you for having convictions — that you know your own mind and are willing to stand up for yourself. So, assert authority by letting your technical expertise and problem-solving ability show.

   But don't go so far as to make flat assertions. Remember, he likes to have things explained and justified. If you say, "No other product in the world can do this," you had better be prepared to justify that statement. If you can't, he'll probably dismiss it as exaggeration.

5. *Keep the customer in a Q4 posture, and be careful not to push him into Q1, Q2, or Q3 behavior.* It's nice to think this customer will remain reasonable, logical, and attentive, but that's not necessarily true. His behavior may change, especially if you provoke the change. A snide or belligerent remark could push him toward Q1 behavior ("I'm not going to let this salesperson get away with that."). Unnecessarily personal probing could push him toward Q2 behavior ("That's none of his business."). Too casual a manner could push him toward Q3 behavior ("I have a joke that is funnier than his.").

6. *Use whatever probes are called for, but rely on open-end probes and summary statements.* To encourage involvement and to keep

from "crowding" the customer, make heavy use of open-end probes. To let him know he's getting through and to check your own understanding, rely on summary statements. However, don't overlook the other probes. With this customer, they're all likely to prove useful.

It's very difficult to keep behavior Q4. Yet, that's essential if you're going to conduct an efficient call. By and large, a Q4-Q4 sales call is the most efficient, the one that achieves the most with the least amount of extra effort. So, to keep your customer behaving in a Q4 manner, stay Q4 yourself. Any deviation on your part may trigger a deviation on his.

7. *Be ready to shift your strategy if the customer's behavior changes.* If his behavior veers from Q4, shift to the Q4 strategy on your part that is appropriate.

Summary

For a comparative summary of Q4 strategies for Q1, Q2, Q3, and Q4 behaviors, see Figure 23 (page 160).

A Reminder

Because first-person statements and process checks don't come naturally to most of us, you have to remind yourself to use them, no matter which strategy you're using. They're two of the most helpful communication techniques described in this book.

Both techniques were explained in Chapter 9, but a recap is useful.

First-person statements say, in effect, that the speaker is involved in a problem along with the listener. Thus, they don't blame or belittle. They merely acknowledge the problem, letting the customer know you're "both in it together" and are looking for a solution. For example:

> "Joe, I'm worried about the trouble we've had arranging delivery on those last three shipments. It's meant extra cost for your receiving department and for our shipping department. What can we do about it?"

Overall Q4 Strategy Guidelines

Q1 Customer Behavior

- Stress benefits to satisfy esteem and independence — status, prestige, autonomy, control, and freedom of action.
- Expect anger, belligerence, sarcasm, skepticism, flat assertions, impatience, and multiple objections.
- Address and vent Q1 anger and probe flat assertions.
- Actions to manage Q1 behavior:
  - Stay cool, and don't let the customer think he's getting to you.
  - Show conviction and strength without sounding cocky, argumentative, or aggressive.
  - Don't argue.
  - Make certain the customer doesn't lose face.
  - Let the customer take credit for good ideas — even when they're yours.
- Rely mainly on open-end probes and summary and reflective statements.
- Be ready to shift your strategy if the customer's behavior shifts.

Q4 Customer Behavior

- Stress benefits that provide something new, creative, innovative, pacesetting, experimental, or unusual.
- Expect the customer to be fully involved, and give him every chance to be.
- By definition, Q4 behavior is task-oriented and reasonable, so expect no behavioral barriers.
- Actions to manage Q4 behavior:
  - Be pragmatic.
  - Be direct and businesslike.
  - Keep the customer in a Q4 posture, and be careful not to push him into Q1, Q2, or Q3 behavior.
- Use whatever probes are called for, but rely on open-end probes and summary statements.
- Be ready to shift your strategy if the customer's behavior changes.

Q2 Customer Behavior

- Stress benefits to satisfy security — stability, low risk, predictability, proven value, and durability.
- Expect the customer to be remote, uncommunicative, hard to read, distrustful, and apprehensive.
- Address Q2 silence, withdrawal, or skepticism.
- Actions to manage Q2 behavior:
  - Be patient.
  - Show genuine concern.
  - Establish trust by using the trust building guidelines we've described.
  - Guide firmly, but gently.
  - Let the customer keep his self-respect.
- Rely mainly on open-end probes, pauses, and brief assertions.
- Be ready to shift your strategy if the customer's behavior changes.

Q3 Customer Behavior

- Stress benefits that provide acceptance, popularity, and a chance to do something other people will appreciate.
- Expect the customer to be enthusiastic and very agreeable.
- Address Q3 enthusiasm, and determine whether agreement is genuine.
- Actions to manage Q3 behavior:
  - Be outgoing and friendly, but don't get sucked into the Q3 whirlpool, or the whole presentation may drown in a sea of irrelevance.
  - Keep the focus on business, but loosen up enough to allow some meandering.
  - Personalize the call.
  - Guide the customer firmly, and make specific suggestions.
- Rely heavily on closed probes and summary and reflective statements.
- Be ready to shift your strategy if the customer's behavior changes.

Figure 23

Process checks are first-person statements for dealing with difficulties in the interactional process itself. They describe whatever is happening to impede the interaction and ask for the customer's help in removing the stumbling block. For example:

> "Maggie, tell me what I might have done to make you insist that you won't answer any questions?"

What's Next?

Earlier, we said that all the concepts and skills that you would learn about Q4 relationship selling apply to a sales manager's job in working with his sales staff. To make our discussion easier to present, we did not cover the manager's role. In the next two chapters, we will specifically relate the Dimensional Model and Q4 techniques to the role of managing — and leading — a sales staff.

CHAPTER 12

Four Ways of Managing Salespeople

If you are a sales manager, you have probably weighed the concepts we have presented in Q4 relationship selling and thought about how your sales force might adapt them to their sales efforts. You may have also thought about how you would convey concepts, such as sizing up a customer's behavior, raising receptivity, learning how to probe, and so on.

How well you are able to teach these skills and how well you relate to your people in general will depend in large part on how well you interact with them. The Dimensional Model can serve just as well in analyzing behavior between a manager and her people as it does in analyzing the salesperson/customer relationship.

For example, you probably would agree at this point that a sales call that is mainly Q1-Q1 will generate a lot more heat than light. Likewise, a coaching session between a manager who displays mainly Q1 behavior with a salesperson who also uses Q1 behavior will probably not accomplish a lot. Similarly, just as a salesperson who glosses over unpleasant topics in a Q3 manner can't expect to produce much understanding and commitment, a sales manager who does the same thing with her people probably won't engender much understanding and commitment either.

In this chapter, we'll take a look at sales manager-salesperson interaction, based on our conviction that the quality of this interaction accounts largely for success in managing people. We'll zero in on the four basic patterns of sales management and their consequences.

Does that mean you should skip this chapter if you're a salesperson? Although we have focused on your selling skills until now, you will probably get more out of these skills if you know how to work well with your sales manager. If you combine your skills with her know-how, the result should be powerful. This chapter will give you some good ideas on how to do it.

The Dimensional Model of Sales Management Behavior

Although we described using this model for one-on-one interactions in Chapter 2, Figure 24 is devoted to the managerial factors of planning, organizing, controlling, and leading. Let's examine each pattern of management in more detail.

Q1 (Dominant-Hostile) Sales Management

We'll hear first from a sales manager who's a firm believer in Q1:

> "Most salespeople must be made to do good work. Without strong prodding, they're almost certain to try to slide by. That's why organizations need managers who can forcefully direct employees into doing the job they're paid to do. In the manager-salesperson relationship, the sales manager should use the power he has. I exercise power openly and without apology. My direct reports understand that there's a payoff if they do things my way. And they also understand that there's a penalty if they don't."

Obviously, this statement of Q1 principles is a caricature. Because it is, however, it highlights some features that distinguish Q1 sales management from other behavioral styles:

1. *Q1 might be called "or-else" sales management.* The message to people is, "Do it my way, or else." The idea is to use power, directly or subtly, as a basic management tool.

The Dimensional Model of Sales Management Behavior

Dominance

Q1 Management Behavior

Planning: Rarely involves salespeople ("Why should I? Planning is my prerogative. I make the plans; they carry them out. That's as it should be.").

Organizing: Tight organization. Patterns of relationship emphasize one-to-one interaction ("I make sure everyone knows what to do and how to do it. I call the shots.").

Controlling: Very close supervision ("Any sales manager who isn't vigilant is asking for trouble. Salespeople must know they're being closely scrutinized.").

Leading: Pushes, demands, drives ("Most people want a strong leader to tell them what to do. My people know who's boss.").

Q4 Management Behavior

Planning: Consults salespeople whenever their thinking might help ("I want the best plans possible. That frequently requires ideas from others. I don't have all the answers.").

Organizing: Patterns of relationship designed to stimulate collaboration and interdependence ("I try to get synergism through pooling of resources.").

Controlling: Tries to develop salespeople who control themselves ("Get people committed to their goals, and they'll supervise their own efforts."). Provides more structure for those who can't.

Leading: Tries to make salespeople aware of their potential ("Leadership is helping people do what they have it in them to do. A leader develops people.").

Hostility — Warmth

Q2 Management Behavior

Planning: Relies heavily on own manager ("I prefer to pass along her plans. That way, my people know they'd better follow through."), or leans heavily on tradition ("It's worked before; it should work again.").

Organizing: Patterns of relationship vague, indefinite. Doesn't encourage interaction ("Just do your own job, and stay out of trouble.").

Controlling: Sees self mainly as a caretaker ("I'm paid to keep things stable. I exert enough control to make sure nobody disrupts routines. There's no point in doing more.").

Leading: Passive, indifferent. Downplays own influence ("Don't kid yourself. No matter how hard you try to lead people, they'll end up doing pretty much as they please.").

Q3 Management Behavior

Planning: More concerned with generalities than details ("If you fence people in with too much planning, you'll demoralize them. I'm flexible; I give my people plenty of leeway.").

Organizing: Patterns of relationship emphasize loosely structured sociability ("If people feel good about their jobs, they'll do their best without lots of regulation. My job is to make sure they feel good.").

Controlling: Relies on high morale to produce hard work ("Control is secondary. What salespeople need most is a good feeling about their jobs.").

Leading: Believes optimism and encouragement get results (Being a sales manager is like being a cheerleader. You can't let your people get discouraged.").

Submission

Figure 24

2. *Q1 sales management is usually a solo performance.* The sales manager runs the show, seeking little help or advice from his salespeople. He makes his own decisions, delegating as little responsibility as possible. When he does delegate, he micro-manages. Communication is mostly one-way: He talks, you listen.

3. *Q1 sales management is not simply a matter of threats, implied or otherwise.* It also uses inducements. The salesperson always gets two simultaneous messages: "If you don't do it my way, you could be in trouble," and "If you do it my way, I'll take care of you." The sales manager is asking the salesperson to trade autonomy in exchange for security. Some salespeople see this as a good bargain, but others don't.
4. *Q1 sales management is generous with punishments, but stingy with rewards.* A salesperson who makes a mistake is almost certain to be blamed or disciplined. A salesperson who turns in a good performance may never hear a word about it.

   This has a distorting effect on the development of a sales force. The frequent use of punishment will certainly reduce the amount of unwanted behavior. But meager use of rewards means that desirable behaviors aren't encouraged. Without encouragement, they may languish and finally disappear. Healthy development requires a judicious and balanced use of both positive and negative reinforcements, rather than the imbalance of Q1 behavior.
5. *Q1 sales management is more concerned with ends than means.* What matters are results. How they're obtained is less important. The sales manager may badger his troops, stretch rules, and ignore policies to get results, but he feels it is worth the trade-off. He sees himself as a "can-do" leader.

Q2 (Submissive-Hostile) Sales Management

A sales manager who practices Q2 behavior might explain herself this way:

> "Too many sales managers have inflated notions of what they can accomplish. I try not to kid myself. I know I'm very limited in what I can do to motivate a sales force. The truth is that most salespeople go their own way. Some are good workers, some aren't. Either way, there's not much their boss can do about it.
>
> "A big part of my job is to keep salespeople from creating turmoil in the organization. Organizations function best without

disruption. To keep things going smoothly, I must let my people know that the top management expects things to be done in a certain way.

"A sales manager must look out for herself. Sales organizations are filled with ambitious people competing with one another. There's politics to contend with, too. Surviving means keeping a low profile and maintaining the status quo. Don't call attention to yourself."

We can derive these features of Q2 leadership from this caricature:

1. *Q2 leadership is pessimistic about people.* Its message is "You can't change the way people work, so why try?" Q2 behavior will not be an initiator of change. Instead, sales managers using Q2 behavior will spend their time looking after the maintenance of their operation and protecting themselves.
2. *Q2 is "pipeline" management, with the sales manager merely serving as a conduit between the people above and those below.* She conveys decisions that are made by a higher authority without providing initiative or personal direction.
3. *Q2 management postpones decisions when possible.* This sales manager feels that putting decisions off is safer than making them. She may make a swift decision if she can get a clear signal as to her boss's preferences. Otherwise, she's likely to procrastinate.
4. *Salespeople in a Q2 setting usually see little of their boss.* When they do, not much happens. She keeps mostly to herself, doesn't say much and is often considered "distant" or "reserved." Her style of communication can best be described as nonexistent, because she avoids talking about work with her people.
5. *Q2 sales management favors traditional, tried-and-true ways of doing things because they are safer than the new or experimental.* The built-in conservatism of Q2 behavior reflects a dislike for taking risks, even calculated ones.
6. *Under Q2 management, salespeople get very little reinforcement, either positive or negative.* Undesirable behavior is seldom punished ("What good would it do?"), and desirable behavior is seldom

rewarded ("What good would it do?"). Because there are never any rewards, this hands-off policy can cause many salespeople to become indifferent and unresponsive.

Q3 (Submissive-Warm) Sales Management

Let's hear from a manager who practices Q3 behavior:

> "The secret of increasing sales is to maintain high morale at all costs, because there's a strong correlation between productivity and morale. As organizations become bigger and more bureaucratic, there's a real danger that humans are ignored. So, to boost morale, salespeople should be treated with warmth, friendship, and an understanding that we're all human and make mistakes.
>
> "That's why I think my most important job as a sales manager is to be friendly, tolerant, and compassionate. Nothing can be gained by pushing or belittling people. I prefer to keep them happy, let them have their way whenever I can, and assure them that I'm in their corner and believe in them."

This caricature points to several features of Q3 sales management:

1. *It's easygoing.* If a salesperson makes a mistake, the manager is likely to overlook it. If a salesperson's productivity is low, the manager will either not say anything or merely speak a few encouraging words of confidence. Q3 management finds it hard to confront unpleasant issues.
2. *Q3 sales management is loose and unstructured.* It has little use for procedures, rules, regulations, systems. The Q3 philosophy is that the job will get done without structure if salespeople are relaxed, happy, and pleased with their jobs.
3. *Q3 sales management is undemanding.* To Q3 management, any demand seems "pushy," as if a manager cannot set high standards without appearing unreasonable to the work force.
4. *In Q3 management, the person in charge dislikes thinking of himself as "the boss."* Whereas Q1 management maximizes the difference between the sales manager and his people, Q3 manage-

ment minimizes it, preferring to be one big happy family.

5. *Q3 sales management hands out positive reinforcement too easily.* The sales manager would rather not talk about unsatisfactory performance. If he refers to undesirable behavior at all, he does it so obliquely and indirectly that the salesperson may not even realize there's a problem.

   Rewarding so easily usually produces confusion. People lose the ability to distinguish between productive and non-productive behavior. This confusion retards or even stifles healthy development.

6. *Q3 management invests much energy in direct person-to-person contact.* Chatting with the sales force about things that have nothing to do with the job — family matters, sports, entertainment, politics, what have you — occupies a disproportionate amount of the manager's time. The Q3 philosophy considers these conversations worthwhile, because they contribute to the harmony considered so vital to productivity.

Q4 (Dominant-Warm) Sales Management

Finally, let's hear from a manager who practices Q4 behavior:

> "As I see it, my job is to get the best out of my sales force, including myself. I must get all my people to see what they are really capable of and how good they could be. I do this by helping them develop the knowledge, skills, and motivation they need to tap their full potential, putting it to work for themselves and the organization.
>
> "My ideal is to develop salespeople who can produce excellent results while exerting a high degree of autonomy and self-direction. However, not every person can be that self-directed. So, in practice, I temper the ideal to fit the individual's capabilities. In the last analysis, management is a matter of coming to grips with individual realities.
>
> "Second, I consider my salespeople as resources for strengthening my own performance. I need plenty of help to get my job done. I believe people have a reservoir of experience, talent, and

ideas that I can draw on to supplement my own. Sometimes, I have to act alone. Whenever possible, however, I would prefer to consult my people and draw on their know-how and insight. If I don't, I'm only cheating myself.

"The net result is that everybody is better off. The people who work for me like being treated as significant contributors to the organization, and this satisfaction pays off in increased motivation. My own performance improves, and the organization gains as a result of their participation."

Let's look closer at Q4 sales management:

1. *Although we're dealing with caricatures, there are sales managers whose behavior approximates the Q4 ideal.* They involve their salespeople strategically in decisions, delegate responsibility, advocate critiquing of performance, encourage two-way communication, and motivate through participation. They may not do these things perfectly, but they try.
2. *Still, some salespeople cannot measure up to the standards of Q4 management.* Most sales managers who believe in Q4 management behavior are realistic. So, they adapt their basic approach to each individual salesperson. When a salesperson can exercise autonomy, she's given the chance. When she can contribute to discussions, she's involved in them. But when she cannot do these things, she's subject to close direction by her manager. Independence and self-direction are for salespeople who can turn them to good use. Those who can't are closely supervised. Q4 management doesn't let the ideal blot out reality.
3. *This leads to one of Q4 management's most important features: It's individualized.* Q4 management is based on the common-sense premise that you can't interact productively with a salesperson unless you know her as an individual. You must know what she wants from her work, what her experience is, what her skills are, what her aptitudes and potential are. You must know her characteristic pattern of behavior, her concerns, and her needs. Only then can you properly customize your interaction with her.
4. *Q4 management welcomes — or at least appreciates — disagreement.*

Q4 management uses disagreement, puts it to work. Q4 management gets disagreement out in the open to see what light it may throw on things. In Q4 management, nothing is beyond discussion. Everything can be questioned, debated, challenged. By exposing weaknesses, disagreement becomes a way of overcoming organizational inertia.

5. *The most basic Q4 idea is that people work best when they have a reason to.* High productivity depends on the sales force understanding the answer to the question "What's in it for me?" Hard, intelligent, efficient work is something people do because they want to, and they want to because they'll get something out of it. Therefore, Q4 management sees to it that each salesperson knows what she'll get out of being productive. Making certain each salesperson understands this is a task Q4 managers take very seriously.
6. *Q4 relationship behavior knows how to develop people.* It makes discriminating use of both positive and negative reinforcements. When justified, however, it emphasizes positive ones. Although it tries to lessen non-productive behavior, its primary aim is to shape productive behavior, because that's the best way to foster growth. Q4 managers use rewards and punishments to fit each particular salesperson.
7. *Finally, and most important, Q4 sales management is practical.* Let's see why:
   - It demands results. Q4 management wants optimal productivity from every salesperson. Q4 management demands the best that people can deliver. It sets tough, exerting goals. It insists on intelligent, analytic handling of problems, and never lets anyone forget that results are what work is all about.
   - Q4 management is realistic about people. It doesn't idealize them, but it doesn't settle for negative stereotypes either ("You can't rely on anybody these days," "Nobody wants to work hard anymore"). In fact, Q4 management doesn't deal with people at all. It deals with each person,

no two of whom are identical. Instead of relying on preconceived notions, Q4 management gets to know each person for what he or she is and then interacts on that basis.

- The manager who practices Q4 behavior is realistic about herself, too. She knows she's human, limited, and very much in need of help. So, she seeks help from her salespeople and from others in the company. Usually, in seeking help, she also gives it. Most Q4 interactions are an exchange of strengths from which both people gain.
- Finally, in Q4 management, the manager is tough on herself. She seeks out help when it's needed, but never abdicates her own responsibility. She doesn't turn over management to her salespeople. She doesn't let popular opinion override her own judgment. She doesn't forget that ultimately she is the one accountable for what happens in her operation. In spite of her belief in involvement, she knows that in the end, she's in charge and nobody else can be.

A Look at the Real World

A legitimate question at this point is: How common are the four patterns of sales management? Does our model of behavior reflect reality? There are two ways to answer this:

1. *Your own experience undoubtedly confirms that all four patterns are very common.* Variants of each can be found in virtually every organization. You can probably recall many instances in which you've observed, interacted with, or yourself displayed each of these behaviors.
2. *Our experience in our own training seminars strengthens the conclusion that the patterns are common.* Participants usually rate their behavior as a mixture of all four patterns, clear evidence that all four are widely used. Our model describes behaviors visible every day in the everyday world.

What's the Payoff?

To answer the question, "What's the payoff?" let's first summarize what we have said about sales management strategies. Figure 25 (page 174) shows the basic attitudes underlying the four patterns and the four ways to carry out management functions.

Figure 25 confirms that, most of the time, you can expect Q4 sales management to pay off better than any other styles of management. That conclusion comes from three sources. The first is behavioral-science research, such as the Ohio State Leadership Studies and studies conducted by Rensis Likert and his colleagues at the University of Michigan Survey Research Center. Second, besides what we have learned from years of consulting with a wide variety of companies, our own specific research among successful managers and those whose careers have derailed supports the idea that Q4 management pays off.

Sixty-seven senior executives, at the level of vice president and higher, were evaluated for success on the job during the research. Each of them had been referred to our firm for training and consultation. The data for the study were extracted from more than 550 feedback surveys. These documents were submitted by the 67 executives themselves, their bosses, and their direct reports

As you would expect, productivity was an overriding concern in the bosses' evaluations of success. After all, they are paid to get results. The study confirms that bosses prefer leaders who place an emphasis on productivity — Q1 and Q4 behavioral styles more than Q2 and Q3.

However, when indicating the type of leader they find most effective, bosses and all other participants in the study chose overwhelmingly those who practice the Q4 style — two to one over those who practice Q1. This suggests that managers practicing Q4 skills are twice as likely to be successful as those practicing the other three quadrant styles of behavior.

When an employee is promoted into a management position, that decision is most likely based on the person's ability and success on the job. What many derailed managers fail to understand is that

Four Ways of Managing Salespeople

Management Function	Q1	Q2	Q3	Q4
Basic attitude	Salespeople must be pushed	Salespeople are what they are	Salespeople produce when happy	Salespeople produce when involved and committed
Planning	Does it on own	Transmits from above	Makes popular plans	Strategically involves salespeople
Organizing	Tightly controls operation	Goes by the book; interaction vague, minimal	Permissive, relatively unstructured	Optimal participation, autonomy, and responsibility for everyone
Controlling	Relies on fear and coercion	Leans on routines	Tends to be lenient and undemanding	Fosters self-control through understanding
Leading	Drives and threatens	Indifferent, distant, unresponsive	Eager to please, appeases, smoothes over	Aware, assertive, responsive, guiding
Decision-making	Does it on own	Delays or follows custom	Compromises; seeks happy medium	Strategically involves other people; seeks optimal decision
Motivating	Negative reinforcement	Neither negative nor positive reinforcement	Indiscriminate, positive reinforcement	Appropriate positive and negative reinforcement
Disagreement	Suppresses	Avoids	Smoothes over	Confronts and resolves
Communications	One-way	No-way	Part-way	Two-way

Figure 25

effective management depends on the performance of the people around them. They never fully realize that successful management rests on their ability to influence others to cooperate and participate.

This lack of insight seems evident when, in this same study, autocratic leaders assessed their own performance. First, as a group, the derailed executives were perfectly happy performing in a Q1 manner. Although they recognized that they were practicing an autocratic style of management, they saw no reason to change. They failed to notice anything detrimental about their style of behavior, although their bosses and direct reports saw it as dysfunctional.

Derailed executives operate under another misconception. They tend to overestimate their management abilities. Although their bosses rated them average or higher on management practices, the derailed executives consistently rated themselves significantly higher. Keep in mind that bosses didn't appear to have a problem with their derailed executives' job-skill levels. This would suggest that their dissatisfaction was with behavior. In other words, bosses weren't unhappy with what these executives do, but rather with the way they do it.

The third way to decide whether Q4 management pays off is your own common sense. This is especially important. Although our own conclusion about Q4 is solidly grounded in both research and experience, it cannot be proven scientifically in the way the boiling point of water can be. Real proof is conclusive. It closes off debate.

Our conclusion is open to debate. We can't prove in the scientific sense that one kind of management will unequivocally be more productive than others. On the whole, however, we think you'll agree that our conclusion meets the test of common sense, and, although common sense doesn't prove anything, it is very convincing.

Let's see, then, why Q4 management can be expected to pay off best by judging it in relation to the seven end-results for which sales managers are usually held responsible. (Figure 26 sums up our conclusions.)

Four Ways of Managing: What's the Payoff?				
End Results	**Q1**	**Q2**	**Q3**	**Q4**
Sales production	High to average with time	Low	Low	High
Cost of sales	High to average	High to average	High	Average to low
Morale	Low	Low	High	High
Employee turnover	High	Low	Low	Average
Teamwork	Low	Low	Low	High
Innovation	Low	Low	Low	High
Development of salespeople	Low	Low	Low	High

Figure 26

These seven end-results are:

1. *Sales production.* However measured, sales usually improve under Q1 management, at least initially. This isn't surprising, because Q1 management is hard-driving. Eventually, however, sales may decline because competent salespeople leave, and the manager fails to develop and tap potential. Consequently, sales under Q1 management are often high in the short run, but only average in the long run.

   Under Q2 management, sales frequently decline or hover below the norm. This is what you would expect when the manager doesn't really believe in leadership and doesn't make a serious effort to assert it. Under Q3 management, sales usually stay below the norm, because problems are ignored or played down. Sooner or later, this refusal to confront harsh reality exerts a toll. Under Q4 management, sales generally go up or stay above the norm.

2. *Cost of sales.* Q1 costs usually rise or remain high. The loss of competent salespeople, the elimination of good ideas and the resentment that Q1 sometimes generates — these all carry a high price tag.

Q2 costs also rise or remain high. Bureaucratic procedures may help keep expenditures in line, but the failure to develop new and better ideas tends to drive up costs. Q3 costs generally rise. Loose organization, unwillingness to say no, and neglect of festering problems are all expensive. Under Q4 management, with its emphasis on optimal productivity and the full use of resources and innovation, costs are average to low.

3. *Morale.* Under Q1 management, morale is usually low, because salespeople resent being stifled or treated like children. Under Q2 management, morale is usually low, because many salespeople are disheartened by the lack of challenge and excitement. A lackluster environment often breeds a lackluster performance.

   Under Q3 management, morale is usually high. Many salespeople find Q3 management very congenial, although some are put off by the lack of decisive leadership. Under Q4 management, morale is usually quite high, especially among those salespeople with the most potential. They like the stimulation and challenge.

4. *Employee turnover.* Q1 turnover is generally high. Frequently, the most capable salespeople don't like being pushed around and often go elsewhere.

   Q2 turnover is generally low. Many people find Q2 management easy to work under ("The boss doesn't bother me; she just leaves me alone."). Under Q3 management, the situation is somewhat the same. Many salespeople like the atmosphere ("I work for a really nice person."). Both Q2 and Q3 managers frequently retain ineffective salespeople because managers don't want the hassle or don't have the heart to let them go.

   Q4 turnover is generally average. Some salespeople don't measure up to Q4 standards. Others can't work for someone who consistently challenges them. Q4 turnover differs from Q1, however. Under Q1 management, turnover occurs mainly among those who want to meet a demand for excellence but find themselves stymied by heavy-handed management. Under

Q4 management, turnover occurs mainly among those who cannot or will not meet the manager's demand for excellence. Thus, Q4 management turns over mostly weaker salespeople, whereas Q1 management turns over stronger salespeople.

5. *Teamwork.* In the strictest sense of the word, there's no such thing as Q1 teamwork. Either the manager runs the team with an iron hand, dictating conclusions that are obediently ratified, or the team is divided by bickering, backbiting, grandstanding, and game-playing.

   Q2 teamwork is also a misnomer. Lacking strong leadership, the team goes through the motions of working together, but that's about all. Q3 teamwork is too relaxed, disorganized, and unbusinesslike, usually delivering poor results. Q4 teamwork is the real thing: goal-directed, businesslike, collaborative, candid, spirited, and effective.

6. *Innovation.* Q1, Q2, and Q3 patterns of management stifle innovation, each in a different way. Q1 management discourages it by "tell-and-do" tactics ("When I want your opinion, I'll ask for it."). Q2 management shies away from anything new or unusual ("Let's stick to what we know."). And Q3 management pays lip service to new ideas, but backs away from implementing any that might create conflict or discomfort. Q4 management seeks out workable new ideas and tries to put them to use.

7. *Development of salespeople.* Domineering Q1, fatalistic Q2, and easygoing Q3 patterns of management all retard development. If any development occurs, it occurs in spite of, rather than because of, the Q1, Q2, or Q3 patterns of management. Q4 management, on the other hand, fosters growth by giving salespeople a chance to perform at their highest level. It helps them discover their own potential and acquire the skills for fulfilling it.

A Caution

One thing to keep in mind about any style of behavior you choose, whether Q4 or not: It's impossible to predict future sales figures, turnover, costs, morale, and so forth in your organization simply on the basis of changing your managerial behavior.

Obviously, many other factors that have nothing to do with managing strategies will affect the outcome. Your style may not be able to overcome the forces of a weak economy, an inferior product or service, financial troubles, a labor strike, or other very real problems. Our point has been that, when other factors are held constant, managerial behavior does have a discernible influence on end results.

What's Next?

Having an effective managerial style does not automatically translate into leading your sales force to greater success. You need to motivate them by using motivational techniques that work. Chapter 13 will tell you what they are.

CHAPTER 13

Motivating Salespeople

A salesperson who reports to you may understand his job. He may know what he's supposed to do and how to go about it. As a sales manager, however, your concern is ultimately with the results he achieves. And results are often a matter of how motivated your people are to perform. In fact, a big part of your task as a leader is to answer the question, "How can I do a better job of motivating my people?"

What is it that drives one person to put in the effort to meet his sales goals, whereas another person slides by or accepts a lot less? What can you do to make your salespeople eager to reach their sales goals? This chapter focuses on how to motivate your people and, equally important, setting performance standards.

Before answering these questions, however, we have to be clear in stating that the skills described in this chapter cannot do the whole job of motivating salespeople. To do all of it, a manager must have other things going for him, such as a good sales compensation program, an accurate feedback system, and effective training. When these factors are in place and the techniques described in this chapter are added, strong motivation should result. But if any of these factors is missing, motivation may be impaired. What ultimately motivates salespeople is the climate in which they work, not just skills. Although necessary, the skills can't do the job alone.

What Is Motivation?

We discussed motivation for customers in Chapter 5. Now, let's review some of the same ideas for your sales force.

Motivation is a "drive to achieve a goal." The motivated person wants to reach a given objective and to do what's necessary to make it happen. Motivation is not the actual achievement. It's putting out the effort needed to achieve. So, a motivated person may not actually succeed, but he'll certainly try.

But why should anyone exert himself at all? What gives people the drive to achieve goals? Simply stated, when people reach a goal, they expect to be better off than they are now. Once achieved, the goal should provide some satisfaction they now lack or more satisfaction than they're already enjoying. Goals that don't promise satisfaction do not motivate.

A motivating goal, then, gives a person an incentive, a reason to exert himself on the job.

Two Kinds of Job Goals

There are two different kinds of job goals:

1. *Business job goals.* These are the ends an employee is expected to attain. They're what he's paid to achieve.
2. *Behavioral job goals.* These are the means to business job goals. They're what the employee must do to attain his business job goals.

Think of it this way: Business job goals are the destination at the end of the road. Behavioral job goals are the road's paving stones that you lay down to get there.

Here's a statement that reflects both goals: "Before you can reach this year's sales quota *(business goal),* you must learn how to manage your time better" *(behavioral goal).* Here are some more examples:

- Business job goal — Increase the unit sales of the large product size during the first quarter of the year by two percent more than unit sales during the last quarter of the last year.
- Behavioral job goal — Practice using reflective statements for venting customer X's negative emotions, so that the next time she loses her temper, you don't lose control of the call.

Note that business goals always focus on the external environment, whereas behavioral goals always focus on the salesperson. Also, business goals are usually more precise, more easily measured.

Q4 Job Goals

A Q4 job goal is any job objective, business or behavioral, that aims at optimal results for everyone concerned, including the employee to whom it's assigned, his manager, and their organization. The purpose of a Q4 job goal is to help everyone be a winner.

Let's examine the crucial phrase, "optimal results." An optimal result is the best result you can get under the circumstances. It's not the ideal result, which would be the best possible result. An ideal result is the highest possible achievement in a perfect world. Optimal results, on the other hand, are real results that come as close to the ideal as possible.

Every Q4 job goal reflects two principles of Q4 management:

1. *We're going after what's realistically attainable.* In the light of everything we know or can anticipate, what's the most we can expect to achieve?
2. *"Realistic" doesn't mean we are looking for excuses to scale down our expectations.* We just want to know what's actually achievable. Once we know, we'll strive toward it, and we won't be satisfied unless we reach it.

What Makes a Q4 Job Goal

A Q4 job goal meets five criteria:

1. *The goal is practical.* A practical job goal can be achieved without obstructing progress toward other goals. For instance, it might

be a goal for a business to increase the number of accounts it has. However, it turns out that going after company X as a new account would require such an inordinate amount of money and effort, it would be unprofitable in the end.

Thus, that particular new account goal, although certainly achievable, would be impractical, because it obstructs the goal of making a profit. It fails the first test of any Q4 job goal: Is it practical? Is it worth the effort? In this case, achieving the goal creates more problems than it solves. A Q4 goal should be a desirable goal, which means it should not get in the way of other equally important or more important goals.

2. *The goal requires optimal effort.* A Q4 goal is neither too hard nor too easy. Several points will clarify what we mean:
   - An easy goal poses little difficulty or challenge. Contrary to popular opinion, research supports the idea that many people want to be challenged. They like pushing themselves to excel. So, these people may be turned off by easy job goals. They become bored and demoralized. Every organization has probably lost people worth keeping because their jobs had become dull or mechanical. Challenging goals might have kept them on board.
   - Understand, however, that there's a big difference between challenging goals and goals that are too hard. A goal is too hard if the employee can't reach it, even when she stretches. Faced with what is perceived as an impossible goal, most people either give up quickly or stick with it only because they don't like to give up. However, this latter group will become increasingly frustrated as they strain to succeed. Their tension builds, and mistakes increase.
   - Paradoxically, then, both extremes lead to the same result: Goals that are too easy or too hard produce discomfort and demoralization.
   - The solution is optimal goals, requiring the right amount of exertion and stress. They stimulate extra effort, but not hopelessness. They require stretching, but not breaking.

This doesn't mean optimal effort always falls halfway between no effort and extreme effort. Optimal effort lies somewhere between "too little" and "too much," which is not always in the middle. How much effort is optimal depends, then, on the goal and the person to whom it's assigned. A goal may be "tough, but achievable" for one person, but "impossible" for another person. To set optimal job goals, you must know your people.

3. *The job goal is specific.* Vague goals cannot produce optimal results because they don't spell out what "optimal" means. Goals such as "Increase sales as much as possible, " "Improve your product mix," or "Trim sales expenses as far as you can," are vague because there's no way to tell for certain if or when they've been achieved.

   These goals aren't even operational. They can't be acted on intelligently. How can you plan to increase sales "as much as possible" unless you know how many sales are possible? We have to guess at the meaning of words like "as much as possible" or "improve" or "trim," because they mean little by themselves. They don't represent an objective measurement. If you state a goal so vaguely, at what point can anyone determine that the goal has been achieved?

   To be usable, goals must be quantified or specified. For example:

   Vague: Slash selling costs to the bone.

   Specific: Slash selling costs by $100 a week.

   Vague: Balance your calls each day.

   Specific: Make four calls on category A accounts and four calls on category B accounts each day.

4. *The job goal is comprehensive.* A Q4 goal tells the whole story, fully describing what's to be achieved, including dates, times, quantities, and other essential details, as well as the conditions of achievement.

   After all, there are certain conditions, limitations, or restrictions to which people are subject when they're pursuing goals. If bounds are exceeded, the goal may be met, but it won't produce optimal results. If these conditioning factors aren't spelled out as part of the goal, you may be asking for trouble later on.

For example, here's a goal that could cause problems, because it's not comprehensive:

> "Cut selling costs in the Northeastern territory by 1.5 percent during the next fiscal year."

This sounds comprehensive. After all, it spells out what's to be done ("cut selling costs"), where ("in the Northeastern territory"), how much ("1.5 percent"), and when ("during the next fiscal year"). What, then, is wrong with it?

Although it tells much of the story, it doesn't specify the conditions under which the goal must be met. For example: A salesperson might cut selling costs by 1.5 percent by refusing to call on accounts on the far edge of his territory, thereby reducing his travel expenses. Would that be acceptable? Or is one of the conditions of the goal that all current accounts be retained while selling costs are cut? If so, the goal should say so. For example:

> "Cut selling costs in the Northeastern territory by 1.5 percent during the next fiscal year, while retaining all current accounts and maintaining or improving this fiscal year's dollar volume of sales to those accounts."

Job goals are most commonly incomplete because the conditions under which they must be met aren't spelled out. We call these conditions or boundaries "contingencies," because the achievement of the goal is contingent on them. When contingencies are omitted, a goal may be achieved in ways that were never intended. After all, anyone can cut selling costs by staying in bed all day. To avoid such surprises, make every job goal comprehensive.

5. *The job goal is understandable.* Several guidelines will help:
   - Word the goal so the salesperson can understand it. It's all right to use technical terms or jargon, as long as they're clear to the salesperson.

- Don't worry if the goal sounds legalistic. This may be unavoidable. After all, like legal language, optimal goals are designed to tie up loose ends.
- Use several sentences instead of one, if it helps clarity. No rule says a goal must be covered in one sentence.
- Include what and when, but not how. Obviously, the salesperson should know how to achieve the goal, but this belongs in a separate plan of action, not in the goal itself.
- Use adjectives and adverbs sparingly. Most adjectives (e.g., fast, slow, high, low, good, bad, satisfactory, unsatisfactory) and most adverbs (e.g., more, less, quickly, slowly) are too vague. If you use an adjective or adverb, make certain it's precise. If it isn't, try to replace it with numbers or some more exact expression. For example, replace "more" with "two percent."

The Behavioral Q4 Job Goal

So far, we've discussed business job goals. Can behavioral job goals also meet our five criteria? Yes.

1. *Practicality.* Any goal that requires a salesperson to change her behavior or improve her skills is impractical if she's unable or unwilling to do it.
    - Unable — You can't get someone to change if it's beyond her capacity. Suppose one of your salespeople becomes very nervous before a presentation. As a result, her presentations are garbled and disorganized. You can assign her this goal: "Overcome your nervousness before presentations so that you come across more convincingly." But that may be beyond her. If she cannot overcome nervousness, the goal is impractical. It's not that nervousness can never be surmounted, but for some people it may seem that way. If so, then, for them the goal is impractical.
    - Unwilling — A behavioral job goal is impractical if a salesperson isn't motivated to achieve it. This doesn't mean it can't be achieved under any circumstances. Q1 tactics may

compel achievement. But don't look for commitment unless the salesperson wants to achieve the goal. If she doesn't, all the Q1 pushing in the world may not help.

2. *Optimal effort.* What we've said about effort regarding business job goals applies to behavioral ones as well. Let's explore the three possibilities:

   - Easy changes in behavior — There's nothing wrong with asking a salesperson to make easy changes in behavior or to adopt easily acquired skills if they'll improve her work. However, most behavioral job goals aren't easy. Most require changing ingrained, habitual behavior that seems second nature. Such changes aren't easy.

   - Extremely difficult changes in behavior — These generate either apathy ("I can't do it, so why try?") or frustration ("I'm sick and tired of trying and failing."). We all do certain things that for all practical purposes cannot be changed, or can be changed only at a prohibitive cost in time and effort.

     This is especially true of certain kinds of expressive behavior. Expressive behavior includes all the ways we express ourselves to other people, either by speech, writing, or gesture. Much of our expressive behavior can be changed. In fact, we've described some ways to do it through probing, the use of presentation skills, and so on.

     However, certain kinds of expressive behavior are extremely difficult to change. Someone who stammers when excited, for example, may be unable to stop doing so without intense effort and, perhaps, professional coaching. Someone whose voice cracks while feeling pressure may be unable to do much about it. Likewise, it's difficult for someone to erase traces of a foreign accent.

     Similarly, no matter how hard they try, certain people cannot acquire certain skills. They lack the aptitude, intelligence, physical dexterity, or whatever else is required. Even when motivated to change, they can't.

This brings us to a key point: A behavioral job goal is legitimate only when it furthers the attainment of a business job goal. Thus, some of the behavioral goals we've just discussed may not be legitimate. Does it really matter in attaining a business goal if a salesperson stammers occasionally or her voice cracks? Will the bottom line be affected if she speaks with a foreign accent? If not, then these behavioral goals should be dropped.

- Optimal changes in behavior — Realistic behavioral job goals that require exertion usually produce the best results. Choose goals that require people to stretch without tearing themselves apart.

3. *Specificity.* Most behavioral job goals cannot be as specific as business job goals. But they can be reasonably precise. Here's an example:

   Vague: Patch up your differences with Fletcher in production.

   Precise: Get Fletcher in production to understand that you're not trying to push him out of his job and that you haven't done anything to undermine him, so that sometime in the next 30 days he agrees to give you shipping information on the telephone again.

   To make behavioral goals reasonably specific, follow these three guidelines:

   - Spell out what will happen if the goal is met. By doing this, you and the salesperson can know if and when the goal's been achieved. The previous example clearly states what will occur if the goal is met (". . . so that sometime in the next 30 days he agrees to give you shipping information on the telephone again.").

     In other words, because a behavioral job goal is legitimate only when it furthers the attainment of a business job goal, state the business job goal. Or, at least, state the business consequence as part of the behavioral job goal. If you cannot link the behavioral goal to a business consequence, the goal is not legitimate and should be discarded.

- When you can, include a deadline. Try not to leave the goal open-ended. Specify when it must be achieved.
- When you can, quantify the goal. This isn't always possible with behavioral job goals, but, when it is, it should be done.

4. *Comprehensiveness.* Like business job goals, behavioral job goals should include all necessary details — what is to be achieved, when, for what purpose, and the limiting conditions, if any. Here's an example, dealing with the acquisition of knowledge, because many behavioral goals are concerned with acquiring or improving knowledge or skills:

   What is to be achieved: Master the details of the new state insurance code.

   When: By August 15.

   For what purpose: So you can explain it to the district sales force at our September sales meeting.

   Limiting condition: Keep any trips to the state capital for this purpose within your present travel budget.

   Behavioral job goals can and should tell the whole story.

5. *Understandability.* Behavioral job goals sometimes sound clear when they're not. They can mean different things to different people. No one, for instance, can tell what these goals "really" mean:

   - Don't push so hard.
   - Get on the team.
   - Don't get excited.
   - Play it by ear.
   - Have a sense of humor.

   These are flawed goals. They're not specific, they're not comprehensive, and they're not really understandable. They can mean many things, and there's no conclusive way to know what they're supposed to mean. To overcome this problem, make the goal specific by explaining its key terms and tie it to a business job goal. Here's an example:

Vague: Assert yourself.

Specific: Make a point of speaking up at least once in each sales meeting to present your ideas on cutting costs. That way, the rest of the sales force can use them to start cutting expenses.

Essentially, specificity and understandability go together. The more specific, the more understandable.

The Motivation Process

Now that we've looked at the nature of Q4 goals, we're ready for the most important question: How can you motivate salespeople to achieve Q4 goals? To get the answer, let's first look at what happens in motivation:

1. *Motivation is concerned with performance.* When you try to motivate a salesperson, you try to get him to perform more productively — to get more out of the time and energy he spends on the job.
2. *Nobody can be expected to work hard and efficiently (productively) unless he sees a benefit in it for himself.* Most people are motivated to achieve a goal when they believe it will help them satisfy their own needs.
3. *Thus, motivation depends on getting the salesperson to see the link between his job goals and his needs.* Once he sees the link, he'll understand how he can expect to benefit from achieving the goals. And once he understands that hard, efficient work will lead not only to the goals, but also to a personal payoff, he should be motivated to perform productively.

This process can be described in a formula:

$$J + N \rightarrow B \rightarrow P$$

J is the salesperson's job goal, business or behavioral. N is his needs, tangible or intangible. When J and N are linked together, the linkage leads to B, the benefit awareness of "what's in it for me if I achieve the job goal." This awareness should lead to P, productive performance.

Let's take a closer look at job goals, needs, benefit awareness, and productive performance.

Job goals (business or behavioral) are what the organization expects the salesperson to achieve. There's no assurance the salesperson will feel a sense of ownership in his job goals. These goals are designed to help the company fulfill its mandate. That doesn't guarantee they'll have any personal meaning for the salesperson. The fact that the company will be better off once a job goal is achieved doesn't answer the question in every salesperson's mind: Will I be better off?

This point cannot be overstated. By themselves, job goals are likely to be considered external to the salesperson. As long as they are, they're unlikely to generate commitment. And when there's no commitment, productivity is usually low.

Something else is needed to provide commitment. That something else is a link between the job goal (his organization's purposes) and the salesperson's needs (his own purposes). A feeling of commitment to the organization's goal comes when the salesperson realizes that the job goal and his needs are intertwined — that whatever happens to the job goal affects him personally.

As we've stated before, every salesperson manifests two kinds of needs on the job:

1. *Tangible needs* — the substantive rewards people seek from their work, the "things out there" that they work for, such as bigger commissions, a promotion, a larger territory, and so on.
2. *Intangible needs* — the psychological drives that underlie the tangible needs, the security, social, esteem, independence, or self-realization needs that impel salespeople to seek particular tangible rewards.

You can make any job goal meaningful to a salesperson if you can show that it matters to him. Once he realizes there's a benefit in it for him, he'll have every reason to follow through. Follow-through is essential for productive performance. If the salesperson is committed to the goal and has the skills, productive performance should follow, and the goal should be met.

An Important Parallel

Obviously, there's a parallel between what we've just said about motivating salespeople and what we said earlier about motivating customers. Figure 27 summarizes these parallels in motivation side by side.

Two Kinds of Motivation	
Motivating Customers	**Motivating Salespeople**
1. Crystallize the customer's needs.	1. Crystallize the salesperson's needs.
2. Describe the pertinent features and advantages of the product or service you think the customer should buy.	2. Explain the job goal you want the salesperson to achieve.
3. Link the features and advantages to the customer's needs, so he sees the benefit — what's in it for him.	3. Link the job goals to the salesperson's needs, so he sees the benefit — what's in it for him.

Figure 27

Recognizing the Salesperson's Needs

To phrase a benefit statement for a salesperson, you must first know her needs. In the case of tangible needs, this usually presents no problem. People often talk about what they want from their jobs. Many salespeople will spontaneously tell you their tangible needs. If they don't, you can always ask. But most salespeople don't talk about their intangible needs. They either haven't thought much about them or don't know what they are. So, if you ask about them, you may get a blank stare.

This means you must uncover intangible needs for yourself. These needs are submerged beneath behavior. The only clues you have are the circumstantial evidence of what the salesperson says or does. By analyzing this behavior, you can infer the needs. Let's look at the telltale signs. We'll start with security needs, and work our way up the familiar pyramid of needs.

Security (Q2) Needs

These behaviors are strong evidence of security needs:

1. *Diffidence.* Appears to lack self-confidence.
2. *Caution.* He keeps his thoughts to himself.
3. *Neutrality.* Doesn't take sides.
4. *Procrastination.*
5. *Indecision.*
6. *Following the leader.* When dealing with the boss or strong peer, seldom talks back, questions, or voices doubts.
7. *Keeping a low profile.*
8. *Working "by the book."* Follows policies, procedures, rules, and precedents to the letter.
9. *Strong respect for tradition.* Shies away from innovations.
10. *Pessimism.* Likely to bring up reasons things could go wrong.
11. *Dependency.* Seems uncomfortable taking the lead.

You probably won't find anyone with all these behaviors, certainly not at one time. But a salesperson who manifests some or most of them a lot of the time probably has strong intangible needs for security.

Social (Q3) Needs

A salesperson who frequently displays some or most of these behaviors is probably impelled largely by social needs:

1. *Amiability.*
2. *Agreeableness.* Whether sincere or not.
3. *Optimism.*
4. *Talkativeness.*
5. *Meandering.* Doesn't stick to the subject.
6. *Intense loyalty.*
7. *Disorganization.*
8. *Gregariousness.*

9. *Sensitivity to cues.* Very alert to negative cues from others, even subtle hints of displeasure. Responds quickly by changing position.
10. *Compromise.* Will assume role of peacemaker and advocates "splitting things down the middle."
11. *Indecision.* Eagerness to please everybody and offend nobody leads to waffling.

Again, no one is likely to do all these things consistently. But any salesperson who displays some or all of these behaviors a good part of the time is probably motivated largely by social needs.

Esteem (Q1) Needs

These behaviors, especially in clusters, are evidence of strong esteem needs:

1. *Boastfulness.*
2. *Domination.* Wants to be the center of attention. Monopolizes conversations.
3. *Interruptions.* Frequently breaks into the middle of sentences.
4. *Obstinacy.*
5. *Self-aggrandizement.*
6. *Strong views.*
7. *High valuation of status.* Easily impressed by rank and position.
8. *Rarely giving credit to others.*
9. *Strong need to win.* Poor loser, rarely acknowledges he's at fault.
10. *Striving for status symbols.*

A salesperson who displays a sizable number of these behaviors time and again is, in all likelihood, motivated by intangible needs for esteem.

Independence (Q1) Needs

Both Q1 and Q4 behaviors are partly motivated by strong independence needs. However, these needs are expressed differently by Q1 behavior than by Q4 behavior. First, Q1 manifestations of independence:

1. *Argumentative.*
2. *Rugged individualism.* Hard to supervise or control.
3. *Resistance to others' ideas.*
4. *Having fixed positions.*
5. *Constantly bidding for autonomy.*
6. *Poor team player.*

Independence (Q4) Needs

Q4 independence is usually displayed quite differently from Q1 independence:

1. *Self-confidence.* Is self-assured but not cocky.
2. *Collaboration.* Is a good team player, eager to take part in team projects.
3. *Acceptance of help.*
4. *Full disclosure.* Speaks her mind without stacking the deck in favor of her own ideas.
5. *Openness to ideas.*
6. *Ability to work on her own.*

Self-Realization (Q4) Needs

The need for self-realization or developing one's potential can usually be recognized by the following:

1. *Probing.*
2. *Candor.*
3. *Diligence.* A steady, serious worker who seldom squanders time.
4. *Desire for challenge.*
5. *Risk-taking.*
6. *Confronting disagreements.* Acknowledges and discusses differences without rancor.

7. *Sharing ideas.*
8. *Sensitivity.*

Two Cautions

1. *Bear in mind that your salespeople will display different needs at different times.* Deal with those needs that seem uppermost at the time. Yesterday's pressing needs may be less pressing today. Don't expect perfect consistency in behavior.
2. *In a brief period of time, any of us may display more than one need.* A salesperson may be eager to please (evidence of a Q3 social need) and eager to take on a tough assignment (evidence of Q4 self-realization need). If so, you'll have to deal with both needs. Behavior is complex.

A Managerial Predicament

Of course, you can infer your salespeople's intangible needs from observed behavior. But why go to all that trouble? There's a practical answer: If you don't know their intangible needs, you may not be able to motivate them. Let's see why.

Motivating people would be fairly easy as long as you could always satisfy their tangible needs. For example, suppose you ask a salesperson what he wants out of his job, and he tells you he would like to be promoted to district manager. You say, "Okay, close the Ajax account by the end of the month and the promotion is yours." That's fine. But what will your motivation for the next assignment be?

The unhappy fact is that no organization has enough tangible rewards to motivate in this way. You can't bestow a promotion, a raise, a bigger office, or a better territory on everyone who wants one. Tangible rewards are always in short supply.

This is a predicament every manager faces. The demand for the things that make motivation easiest outruns the supply. What can you do about it?

There are four ways to motivate:

1. *Satisfy the salesperson's tangible needs by using tangible rewards when you can, that is, if they're available and if they're deserved.*
2. *At the same time, try to satisfy his intangible needs directly.*
3. *When you cannot fill tangible needs, concentrate on filling intangible needs.*
4. *If it's practical and suitable to do so, satisfy both tangible and intangible needs.* If not, at least satisfy the intangible needs.

You can now see why it's so important to observe and decipher behavior. By paying attention to what a salesperson says and does and then inferring his intangible needs, you establish a fall-back position for motivating him. If you don't have tangible rewards to offer, you can fall back on intangible rewards — if you know his intangible needs.

A Caution

When motivating, remember it's very easy to project our own needs onto other people. When we project, we attribute our own ideas, feelings, or needs to somebody else, although there's no clear evidence that she thinks or feels or has the same needs as we do. We jump to the conclusion that "because I feel this way, she does too." We often do this automatically.

To avoid this trap, make a deliberate attempt to check your conclusions about the salesperson's needs, especially her intangible needs. Once you have concluded, for example, that she has a strong need for self-realization, ask yourself: Do I have evidence? Have I observed behavior that shows she's eager to grow? Or am I assuming she has this strong need for self-realization just because I do?

It's very human to project from time to time. In motivation, it must be resisted. The motivation formula doesn't work unless you address the salesperson's real needs.

Which Benefits Motivate?

Once you know the salesperson's needs, which benefits should you use to motivate? Obviously, we can't provide an exhaustive list, but we can list some of the more obvious benefits, which are presented in Figure 28 (page 200). Note that all the tangible benefits are in limited supply, whereas the supply of intangible benefits is unlimited.

What's Next?

Although motivating salespeople is a vital use of your Q4 leadership skills, you can bring to your management role another Q4 skill that can influence your people and your results in a profound way. That is the ability to develop your people to become the best they can be. We'll discuss coaching in the next chapter.

Which Benefits Motivate?		
Needs	**Tangible Benefits That Are Likely to Motivate**	**Intangible Benefits That Are Likely to Motivate**
Q1 (esteem and independence)	• Bigger salary or commission • Special responsibilities • Special or unusual assignments • Chance to handle "major" accounts • Promotion or special title • Bigger office, new furniture, company car • Freedom from paperwork required of other salespeople	• Compliments • Recognition of achievements, especially official recognition • Involvement in decision-making; opportunity to give advice • Respect
Q2 (security)	• Routine, predictable assignments • Compensation and fringe benefits that bolster security • Chance to work with well-established, long-time accounts • Patience and assurance	• Promises of support as needed • Absence of pressure • Working in closely structured situations • Deserved praise
Q3 (social, esteem, security)	• Frequent opportunities to interact with others on the sales force • Chance to work with easygoing, sociable accounts • Freedom from "detail" work	• Frequent conversations with the boss • Deserved praise • Friendliness; personal touch
Q4 (independence and self-realization)	• Assignments that tap unused ability • Added responsibility • Promotion to a more challenging job • Compensation tied to achievement	• Opportunity to make "extra" contribution • Candor from boss • Being kept informed • Chance to suggest new ideas • Involvement in decision-making

Figure 28

CHAPTER 14

Q4 Coaching for Success

What's the most important thing a sales manager can do as a leader to make a difference among his people? Help them to develop. That's right, applying Q4 skills in the most effective way not only motivates your sales staff, the net result is that they develop in their roles. Their skills increase. All other factors being equal, this will translate into greater selling success.

Effective development requires a lot of skill. It is not easy. One of the best and most available tools you have for developing people is coaching. This chapter explains how to coach effectively and how to overcome the obstacles that frequently arise while doing it.

Let's start with an informal definition of what we mean by coaching. Coaching is any talk between a sales manager and a salesperson that's intended to help the salesperson do a better job.

The talk may take place in a car between sales calls, over a cup of coffee, by telephone, in a lobby while waiting to see a customer — whenever it's timely and convenient. The "curbstone conference" is a good example, in which the manager and the salesperson stand on the sidewalk and talk about the last sales call. The whole idea of that informal get-together is to help the salesperson do even better. We say "even better" because coaching isn't meant just for salespeople who are doing poorly. It's for all salespeople, even the best, based on the principle that there's always room for improvement. It's the sales manager's job to guide the salesperson toward that improvement.

Methods of Development

It's important to note that coaching is not the only effective technique for developing salespeople. Day-by-day management, formal training courses, and performance appraisals are also important. Before we proceed, let's position coaching in context with these other methods.

1. *Day-by-day management.* Your day-in, day-out interactions with a salesperson are a potent development technique. Whether intended or not, everything you say and do conveys a clear message: "This is the way I think it should be said and done." Thus, even when you are not aware of it, you're a role model.

   Beyond that, you can deliberately convert these encounters into short but effective training sessions. How? Apply the Structured Sales Call Format as described in Chapter 10. By involving the salesperson and making her think, you are providing a catalyst for development.

   This is a major difference between Q4 and Q1 management. Because Q1 management imposes and dictates, it doesn't engage the mind of the other person. It doesn't lead to self-discovery, the "Aha!" reaction. Thus, the Q1 approach is more likely to stifle development than foster it. Q4 management engages the mind. It helps the salesperson actualize her potential, that is, converting what could be into what is. That's the essence of development.

2. *Formal training.* Formal training means taking courses, workshops, seminars, and classes either on or off the job. There are usually two categories: courses that impart information and courses that develop skills.

Unhappily, some sales managers equate all training with formal training. As soon as they spot a training need, they search for a course being offered to fill it. They may be disappointed.

Why? Because even if a suitable course is available, it is often difficult to develop skills quickly and efficiently. Skills rarely develop right away. A good course is a starting point, providing the insight and know-how for building skills, but the actual building takes time, follow-through, and practice.

So, although formal training may be a springboard to better performance, following it up with perseverance, support, and feedback is essential or the improvement won't materialize.

3. *Performance appraisal.* In an annual performance appraisal, manager and salesperson formally discuss the effectiveness of the salesperson's performance since her last appraisal, why performance has been effective or ineffective, and how she can make it more effective in the coming period.

   An effective appraisal can be used to help the salesperson acquire insight into her performance. The manager guides the appraisal, but doesn't impose her ideas unless the salesperson cannot or will not figure things out on her own. The idea is to help the salesperson grow during the appraisal and after.

4. *Coaching.* As we've said, this is the manager's most available tool for developing salespeople. There's no need to wait for a formally scheduled time or designated place. There's no need for a special budget. A manager who can't afford formal training can afford coaching. It's always there to be used as needed.

Coaching: What It Is

Coaching puts the prime responsibility for training where it belongs, on the field sales manager. An outside seminar can help, as can the training department. However, most development must happen while the salesperson is on the job. This means the person in regular contact with the salesperson, the manager, can most significantly affect her development.

Let's define coaching in a way that isolates its major components.

> A discussion (1) initiated by either salesperson or sales manager (2) whenever either deems it advisable (3) in which both people analyze some aspect of the salesperson's performance, behavior, or attitudes on the job and (4) to change, maintain, or improve the performance, behavior, or attitudes.

Now, let's take it in its simple components:

1. *Coaching and counseling can be initiated by either manager or salesperson.* Usually, the manager does the initiating, but not always. Anytime a salesperson says something like, "I'm having trouble with the Ajax account; can we talk about it?" he's initiating a coaching session, whether he knows it or not.
2. *Coaching can happen whenever either party thinks it's needed.* There are no set times for it. It happens because either manager or salesperson thinks it will help.
3. *In coaching, both people analyze some aspect of the salesperson's performance, behavior, or attitudes.* This differs from performance appraisal, which analyzes not just one aspect, but all of what the salesperson is doing. Performance appraisal seeks an overall view of performance, whereas coaching zeroes in on one part.
4. *The purpose of coaching is to reinforce sound behavior or attitudes so they're maintained and to examine ineffective behavior or attitudes so they can be changed or improved.* Coaching aims at optimal productivity.

With these four features in mind, we're ready for an even fuller definition:

> Coaching: is (1) the use of managerial insight and know-how (2) to elicit self-analysis by the salesperson to deepen his understanding of the job he's doing and why (3) to get his commitment to maintain or improve what he's doing, and get his commitment to applicable goals and action plans.

Let's look at the three added features of our new definition:

1. *Coaching requires managerial insight and know-how.* Your responsibility is first to know enough about the salesperson's work to

offer useful guidance and advice. After all, you can't coach someone on how to probe an uncooperative customer unless you yourself know how. Second, you must know enough about human behavior to help the salesperson understand her attitude problems or interpersonal problems, if she has any. Third, you must know how to raise receptivity, probe, and motivate.

2. *At its best, coaching elicits self-analysis by the salesperson.* Instead of telling her what her problem is or how to solve it, you help her discover these things for herself. This doesn't always work. When it doesn't, you have no choice but to tell her what she needs to know. Still, the aim of Q4 coaching is to encourage as much self-discovery as the salesperson can attain.
3. *Q4 coaching seeks not just understanding, but also commitment to performance goals and plans.* It relies heavily on the motivation formula we've described.

Coaching and Performance Appraisal

With a clear understanding of coaching in mind, we can now present our guidelines for Q4 coaching. With minor modifications, they can also be used to conduct Q4 performance appraisal. Although coaching and performance appraisal are different activities, they use the same techniques. Let's make certain the differences are clear:

1. *Performance appraisal is more ambitious.* Coaching deals with just one or several aspects of performance. Its focus is narrow. Appraisal deals with overall performance and, beyond that, provides data the company needs to make optimal use of its human resources, make equitable compensation decisions, comply with government regulations, and set yearly objectives. Thus, performance appraisal is considerably more far-reaching.
2. *Coaching can happen anytime, wherever manager and salesperson find it convenient.* A performance appraisal interview happens only at prescribed times (usually once a year), almost always in the manager's office.

3. *Performance appraisal requires more structure and preparation, whereas coaching sometimes occurs spontaneously, with no preparation beforehand.*
4. *Performance appraisal usually takes longer.* Although there is no rule and it could be longer, a coaching session may last 10 or 15 minutes. An appraisal may take several hours.

Understanding these differences, you can still apply the coaching guidelines to performance appraisal, because both use essentially the same methods and skills.

Coaching: The Foundation

Effective coaching is built on four pillars:

1. *Trust.* Coaching tries to motivate the salesperson to take a particular action, such as improving a skill, maintaining an effective way of working, adopting a better attitude, etc. This requires trust. The salesperson must believe that what you're urging her to do is in her self-interest. Unless she's convinced you have her welfare in mind, the coaching session will probably fail. Without trust, the best you can hope for is grudging submission.

   The best generator of trust is Q4 behavior. A Q4 open, candid, and we-oriented approach is most likely to convince the salesperson that you aren't playing games with her. Several Q4 guidelines are especially important for building trust:

   - Do it every day. This is the basic guideline. You can't turn on trust like a faucet whenever it's convenient. It must be there all the time. If you don't build trust every day, it won't be there on special occasions.
   - Take enough time. You won't convince a salesperson you have her best interests at heart if you hurry through coaching, impatient to get on to something else. If you don't have time to do it right, put it off until you do.
   - Start with a benefit statement. One way to convince the salesperson the session is in her best interest is to tell her at the

start what is in it for her. A clear, believable statement of tentative benefit will help establish trust early.

- Don't carve your ideas in stone. Obviously, you're going to start with some ideas about what the salesperson is doing and should do. But don't treat them as immutable laws. Be flexible discussing your thoughts, and if you become convinced your hypothesis is wrong, change it and admit it. Otherwise, you may create the impression you've rigged the session — hardly a way to generate trust.
- Keep the salesperson involved. A Q4 coaching session is a dialogue, a joint effort to reach understanding and commitment. It is not a pretext for beating down the salesperson. If you use Q1 behavior and monopolize the session with only your views, you'll convince her you don't care what she thinks. Trust will go out the window.
- Don't give instant advice. A strong temptation in coaching is to jump right in and say, "I think you should. . . ." Resist it. If the salesperson's receptivity is low, your advice will drive it lower by generating resentment ("The boss doesn't care what I think."). Probe first, increase receptivity, get her views, and then offer your advice.
- Face up to disagreements. Few things will lower trust faster than the suspicion that you're ducking an issue.
- Don't push for total agreement. It's a rare coaching session in which both people see eye-to-eye on everything. Your ultimate goals of understanding and commitment require fairly full agreement, but not a lock step alignment of views. If you can't get complete agreement, settle for partial agreement. Otherwise, you'll wipe out whatever trust you may have built.

2. *Self-analysis and self-discovery.* You are the guide who gets the salesperson to realize for himself what's going on and what to do about it. Because the discovery is his own, it's more credible and persuasive than if it came from you.

However, self-discovery can only come after self-analysis. The salesperson must first think about what he's doing, what the consequences are, what they should be, and so on. To stimulate this analysis, use probes. Ask pointed questions, clear the air of emotions that inhibit logic, give him time to think, and keep the analysis on track. Otherwise, he may never get to those flashes of insight.

Why bother with self-analysis and self-discovery? After all, you can save time by simply explaining his situation to him. There are three good reasons he should figure it out for himself:

- We retain more of what we discover for ourselves, and we retain it longer. When we work to discover for ourselves, the effort seems to etch the discovery into our brains.
- We understand more of what we discover for ourselves. By puzzling-out problems, we see things we would otherwise miss. When we hear the solution from someone else, we hear only the conclusion. If we work out the solution, we go through the steps to arrive at it. That deepens our understanding.
- Self-discovery is more likely to produce a committed change in behavior. A conclusion we reach is one we own and have a stake in. We don't feel ownership of an idea imposed on us. In fact, we may resent it.

Q4 coaching aims at self-analysis and self-discovery, but it sometimes misses the mark. As we will see, some salespeople will not or cannot analyze or discover. Other salespeople do it in only limited ways. Thus, to conduct Q4 coaching, encourage self-discovery when it's feasible and impose your conclusion when it is not. Your imposition need not be heavy-handed or bullying, but it must be firm.

3. *Adaptive tension.* Because Q4 coaching is action-oriented, it means setting a goal or goals for your salespeople to strive to reach. Such a goal demands an appropriate level of energy. The appropriate or optimal energy needed is the golden mean between complacency and stressful tension.

Regulating the optimal level of energy or tension between these two extremes is similar to regulating a thermostat. If it is set too low, there is no tension, no drive to accomplish the task. Of course, if it is set too high, it leads to an unacceptable level of non-constructive tension, which can become too stressful and be a distracting obstruction to performance.

Your goal is to apply the optimal amount of tension that stretches your salesperson and motivates her to put forth her best effort. Constructive tension results in maximum productivity. Figure 29 illustrates what the right amount of tension means to performance.

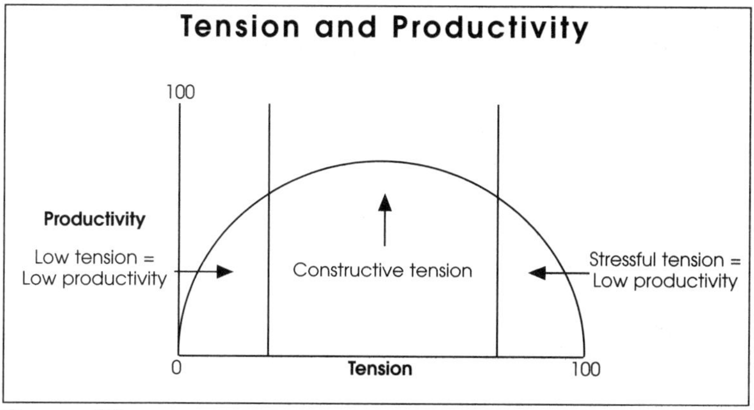

Figure 29

The figure helps us make four generalizations:

- Q1 behavior is on the right of the diagram. These salespeople are operating at a level of non-constructive tension that creates stress. This hurts their own performance, because they are too tense. They view everything as monumental, a crisis. They need to be coached to dial down and learn to operate at a tension level that is motivating and productive, not crippling and destructive.
- Salespeople who have strong Q2 needs are at the left on the diagram. They put forth just enough effort to get by. They need their level of constructive tension raised to improve

sales performance. To change the tension level, they must be confronted in a Q4 manner so they understand that their low-tension mode is adversely affecting their productivity. This can be handled in a firm yet reassuring way.

- Salespeople with strong Q3 needs also need more tension applied. They tend to be easygoing, even lackadaisical. So, their goals should contain both extra constructive tension and structure to make certain they follow through. If the tension isn't structured, it may be wasted.
- Salespeople with strong Q4 needs usually respond to tension well. They like fairly strenuous goals, because these offer the best chance to grow. So build optimal constructive tension into their goals, and give them as much autonomy as feasible.

How much tension is optimal? It is unique to each situation. Setting optimal goals and doing optimal coaching require knowing your people as individuals and knowing how to individualize the use of tension. That's a major part of Q4 management.

4. *The structured coaching format.* Q4 coaching follows its own version of the Structured Sales Call Format. For this reason, we should clarify an earlier point. We said coaching is sometimes done spontaneously. This is because it responds to a need that arises. It may happen suddenly, for instance, when a salesperson walks into your office distraught about a problem. Obviously, that's an impromptu coaching session.

   However, it doesn't mean you should not prepare for coaching when you are able to. The quality of the session is almost certain to be improved if both you and your salesperson do some advance work. When possible, you should:

   - Set the objectives of the session ahead of time.
   - Gather any data you expect to prove useful.
   - Plan the strategy you expect to use during the session. Make certain it fits this salesperson.

- Tell the salesperson about the meeting. Explain why you're setting it up, what data she'll need, and what she should do to prepare. Try to eliminate surprises at the meeting.

So much for preparation. Let's look at the session itself.

A Structured Coaching Process

We said earlier that what happens in Q4 coaching parallels what happens in Q4 selling. Both are structured processes, and in both, the components are basically the same:

Q4 Selling	Q4 Coaching
Open the call	Open the talk
Explore customer needs	Get the salesperson's views
Present your product	Present your views
Manage objections	Resolve disagreements
Close the call	Work out an action plan

A brief description of the five components of Q4 coaching follows.

Start the Talk

You want to ensure two things in this first component: that the salesperson's ready to pitch in and help the discussion along and that he doesn't feel threatened by talking with you as his boss.

To start the talk:

1. *Be suitably sociable.* Do what's necessary to start off on the right foot. For instance, if the salesperson has strong Q2 needs, begin on a low key. If he has strong Q3 needs, chat a little, and so on.
2. *Explain the purpose and benefit.* Tie the benefit to his tangible and intangible needs. ("Jake, let's take a few minutes to examine that last call. That way, the next time a customer starts yelling like that, you can calm him down and save yourself the kind of browbeating you just took.")
3. *Set the ground rules.* Explain how the session's going to work. A good way to do this is to run through the five components very

quickly. That way, the salesperson will understand at the outset the role he's expected to play.

4. *Probe receptivity.* Don't be surprised if he's tense or reluctant. Many people are apprehensive about coaching. They're afraid they'll be blamed or belittled. So, before plunging ahead, make certain he's willing to plunge in with you. If he's not, increase his receptivity.

Get the Salesperson's Views

You have one goal here, to find out what the salesperson thinks about what's being discussed. Why should you care? First, because you may learn some useful information. Second, because you want her to feel committed to any decisions that are reached. She's much more likely to feel committed to a shared decision, not one that's simply yours.

Why get her views at this time? As the boss, if you reveal your viewpoint first, it could suppress or at least color her thinking. So, make certain she talks first.

To get the salesperson's views:

1. *Probe.* To find out what a salesperson thinks, ask her. Start with an open-end probe, and keep on until you get the whole story.
2. *Promote candor.* This is often hard to do, because a lot of coaching deals with people's shortcomings, and the salesperson may not like discussing them. So, instead of getting Q4 disclosure, you may get Q1 bravado, Q2 evasion, or Q3 meandering. Stick with it, dig deep, and don't settle for less than her real thinking.
3. *Withhold your opinions.* Whatever she says, keep your reactions to yourself. Don't jump to conclusions. If she finds out what you think, she may tailor her remarks to please you, and that's not candor.

Present Your Views

You have three goals: respond to the salesperson's ideas; present your own, if they differ; and make certain each of you understands the other.

To present your views:

1. *Tell the salesperson on what you agree.* If you go along with his ideas, say so. If any are good, be certain to give him credit.
2. *Explain on what points and why you disagree.* If some of your ideas differ, explain them without belittling his. Try to prove that your ideas will be good for him, comparable to developing a benefits statement during a sales call.
3. *Summarize.* Once you're certain he understands your views, summarize points on which you agree and disagree. Don't be surprised if there's some fairly strong disagreement. After all, he may take exception if you've been critical. Be prepared for denial, defensiveness, or resentment. Deal with all these by probing.
4. *Get the salesperson's reaction.* Probe to see if he understands and agrees. Watch out for automatic Q2 ("Whatever you say.") or Q3 ("Terrific!") responses. You want real reactions.

Resolve Disagreements

You now want to clear the air of emotions and settle as many of your differences as possible.

To resolve disagreements:

1. *Acknowledge your disagreement by summarizing both positions.* Spell out each issue, every unsettled point ("Regina, as I see it, the question is whether you should have offered the discount so early in the presentation . . . ."). Then summarize where you both stand. Probe to be certain she agrees with the summaries.
2. *Probe the positions.* Probe so the salesperson thinks through her position. Then explain your own. The idea is to expose the pros and cons of both positions. This process will likely spark some heat, as well as light. The salesperson may become defensive, resentful, sullen, even belligerent. Be prepared to vent these emotions. Open-end probes and reflective statements should help. Once both positions have been explored, see whether there's a third or fourth position that's more sound than either.

3. *Settle your differences.* Compare all positions. Pick the one that promises to be most productive for everyone concerned. This may not be easy. If you can't reach agreement, you'll probably want to impose your own position — unless you're not certain what the conclusion should be. In that case, you may want to let the salesperson reach her own conclusion and try it out.
4. *Confirm the decision.* Get the salesperson to voice her understanding of what you've agreed on. If you have to, do this yourself. Either way, make the decision explicit.

An easy way to remember how to resolve disagreements is the term APAC, discussed in Chapter 10, which stands for **A**cknowledge, **P**robe, **A**nswer, **C**onfirm the answer.

Work Out an Action Plan

Now that you've resolved your disagreements, you want to develop several solutions to the original problem and pick the best, devise a plan for carrying it out, and make certain the salesperson understands and buys into both the solution and the plan.

To work out an action plan:

1. *Ask the salesperson to propose some solutions, and pick the best one.* If the solution is one he devises, he'll almost surely be committed to it. Add any ideas you think should be considered. What counts is to come up with the best solution together, regardless of who originated it. Discuss the various proposals, and modify or combine them to come up with the one both of you think will work best.
2. *Make the benefit plain.* Make certain he understands that the solution will be good for him. If it won't be, he will not be likely to follow through on the action plan.
3. *Devise an action plan.* Spell out what's necessary to implement the solution. Let him take as much initiative as he can in developing the plan.
4. *Check understanding and commitment.* Finally, probe to ensure that everything's clear and acceptable, that the salesperson

knows what he's supposed to do and believes in it. If he does, you've just finished a successful coaching session.

To reiterate an important concept: Try to get the salesperson to come to the discovery by himself, but when self-discovery is impossible, impose your own conclusions. If you can, guide him to his own conclusions. If that fails, step in, using a Q4 manner. After all, you're the manager, and you're ultimately responsible for what happens in your operation.

The Interactional Dilemma

In a coaching interaction with a salesperson that calls for the structured format, you want three things to occur:

1. *The salesperson should contribute something — an idea, some information, an insight, a perspective — that will help both of you accomplish more together than alone.* You want the discussion to synergize, producing results greater than the sum of your individual efforts.
2. *The salesperson should discover for herself something she didn't know.* Whatever it is, even with your guidance, she should make the discovery, because you want her to experience the "Aha!" effect.
3. *The salesperson should grow and come out of the session knowing or believing something that will help her do a better job.*

Ideally, these things should always happen in coaching. But what if they don't?

What if the salesperson cannot or will not contribute? What if she lacks intellectual ability or experience? What if she's determined, for whatever reason, to withhold her contribution and undermine the session?

What if she cannot or will not discover things for herself? What if your best efforts never produce the "Aha!" effect?

What if she cannot or will not grow? What if she doesn't want to, preferring to stay as she is? What if she can't grow any more?

In short, what if your Q4 management doesn't produce the synergism, self-discovery, and growth it should? This is the interactional dilemma — having to choose between two unsatisfactory alternatives. In this case, it's a matter of responding in one of two ways:

1. *You can shrug it off and tell yourself that nothing can be done to get results from this person.* "She is what she is, and that's that." This is the Q2 option.
2. *You can impose your own ideas on her, but without anger or hostility.* "I see things differently. Here is what I expect from you." This may sound Q1, but it's not. It's Q4 for these reasons:
   - Your action comes after the salesperson proves unable or unwilling to contribute and achieve self-discovery.
   - Your action is not arbitrary. It's accompanied by a reasonable explanation.
   - Your action is not hostile. It neither blames nor belittles. It's simply an effort to move off dead-center and get the job done.

Which alternative should you choose? The second one — imposing your ideas, but without anger or acrimony. This isn't ideal, but it is realistic. It should produce some results. The alternatives, bulldozing or going along with the status quo, are worse.

To determine how much you need to intercede in developing a salesperson or what her capacity for self-development may be, we can represent an evaluation of development potential graphically by using what we call the GUIDE continuum, which is shown in Figure 30.

GUIDE is an acronym for Growth potential, Understanding, Insight, Desire, and Effectiveness. In deciding where a salesperson fits on the continuum, you must consider:

1. *Growth potential.* How much untapped capacity for growth does the salesperson seem to have?
2. *Understanding.* Is she intellectually capable of synergizing, discovering, and growing?

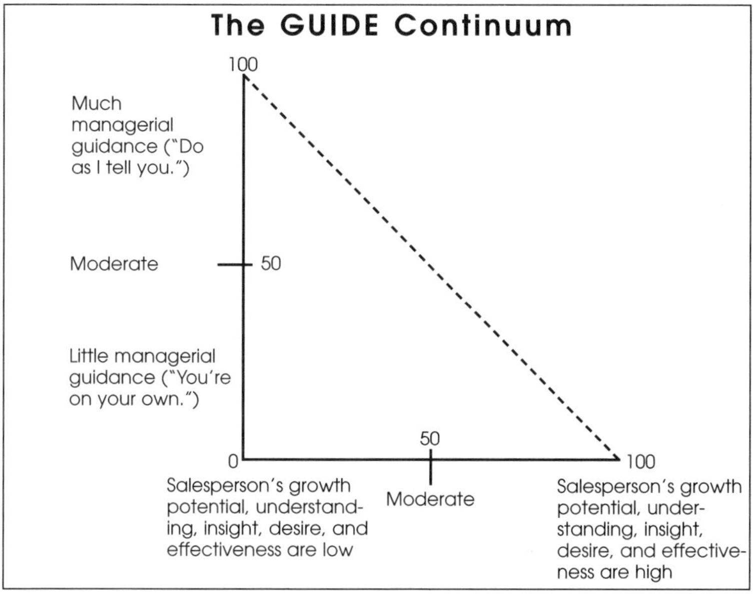

Figure 30

3. *Insight.* Does she have what it takes to see herself as she is?
4. *Desire.* Is she motivated to synergize, discover, and grow? If not, can she be motivated?
5. *Effectiveness.* What's her present level of skill, knowledge, and performance?

The answers will tell you where, in general, the salesperson belongs on the GUIDE continuum. That, in turn, will tell you how much you should guide her, and how much she can guide herself.

The GUIDE continuum helps us explain why different salespeople need different amounts of guidance. It also explains why each has a different capacity for development. Salespeople have different capacities for all five of the GUIDE factors. Their growth potential varies.

The GUIDE continuum is a tool to inform you about how much a salesperson can be expected to develop, how long it might take, and how much of your effort it will require.

A Caution

This doesn't mean you can always predict development accurately. People sometimes confound all predictions. A salesperson who seems headed for dramatic growth may disappoint us, whereas one who seems unable to grow may surprise us. As a sales manager, you must make predictions about people. If you're a fair, careful observer, chances are your observations will be on target.

To be a fair and objective observer, however, it's important not to distort your observations with personal biases. You have to correct your distortions to predict how development will go. Here are two tendencies to keep in mind:

1. *Managers who habitually use Q1 and Q2 behaviors are sometimes unfairly pessimistic about human development.*
2. *Managers who habitually use Q3 behavior may be undeservedly optimistic about human development.*

When using the GUIDE continuum, confront your own biases, as well as the facts.

Q4 Strategies

Not only should the amount of guidance you provide be tailored to the individual salesperson, all the components of effective coaching must be tailored, too. Basically, the strategies are the same for coaching as they are for selling. Dealing with a salesperson's Q1 behavior is like dealing with a customer's Q1 behavior.

Obviously, with a salesperson, you can impose your ideas in a way you cannot with a customer. However, as you know, successful coaching and development isn't just a matter of using your clout. Here, then, is a brief summary of how to tailor your Q4 coaching strategy to deal with the four quadrant behavior patterns your sales staff may exhibit.

The Q4 Strategy With Q1 Behavior

1. *Stress esteem and independence benefits.* Remember that this salesperson doesn't like coaching because it cramps her style and

reminds her that you are the boss. So, it's very important to show her how the session can enhance her self-image and enlarge her freedom.

2. *Vent hostility and probe flat assertions.* You'll probably get a fair amount of both. Be prepared to do plenty of reflecting and digging.
3. *Deal with the salesperson's concerns first.* If she has something on her mind, let her do it before getting to your concerns. Don't make her feel neglected.
4. *Don't get annoyed.* Q1 behavior can be irritating, but if you let it get to you and show it, it'll impair the problem-solving process. Stay focused on your Q4 game plan.
5. *Be strong, but don't use Q1 behavior.* It's self-defeating to answer Q1 behavior with Q1 behavior. Show Q4 strength by speaking with conviction. Assert yourself, but steer clear of flat assertions and Q1 noise.
6. *Rely heavily on open-end probes and summary and reflective statements.* The idea is to manage the discussion without making the salesperson feel boxed in. Use leading and closed-end questions sparingly.
7. *Be prepared to shift your behavior when the salesperson does.* Nobody's locked into Q1 behavior. If your Q4 efforts pay off and her behavior changes, change yours accordingly.

The Q4 Strategy With Q2 Behavior

1. *Stress security benefits.* For this salesperson, coaching means confronting problems, which he doesn't like to do. Also, the mutual resolutions produced by coaching may require changes in behavior that disrupt the comfortable Q2 routine. So, your coaching must convince him he'll end up more secure, not less.
2. *Be patient.* Slow down. If you hurry, you'll only make this salesperson more nervous. You won't teach him much if you put him under strain.

3. *Show genuine interest.* This salesperson needs to be assured that you're really on his side, that you want him to succeed.
4. *Guide firmly but gently.* Aim for self-discovery, but realize that it'll take a good deal of probing on your part. Don't try to save time by pushing him faster than he's able to go.
5. *Stress open-end probes, pauses, and brief assertions.* Don't use leading and closed-end questions. Don't make him feel "cornered."
6. *Adapt your behavior to shifts in his behavior.* If your strategy works, he may loosen up a bit. If you pressure him, however, he may move toward Q1 behavior.

The Q4 Strategy With Q3 Behavior

1. *Stress mostly social, as well as security and esteem, benefits.* Basically, this salesperson will change if she feels other people will be pleased by the changes.
2. *Socialize, but don't overdo it.* There's almost no way to coach this salesperson without engaging in some chitchat, but don't get overtaken by it yourself.
3. *Guide firmly and be specific.* This salesperson needs structure. So, provide well-organized, systematic, and thorough direction.
4. *Don't be lulled.* Probe beneath all the enthusiasm and goodwill that seems to indicate an eagerness to change. You may find some strong doubts and reservations under all that exuberance.
5. *Rely heavily on closed-end questions and summary and reflective statements.* Go very easy on open-end probes and pauses.
6. *Shift your behavior if her behavior shifts.* Nobody's genial and easygoing all the time. Coaching does produce pressures, and these can push Q3 behavior into another quadrant. Be ready.

The Q4 Strategy With Q4 Behavior

1. *Stress self-realization and independence.* This salesperson appreciates coaching and expects a lot out of it. Show him how it'll help him grow and achieve. Otherwise, you'll dampen enthusiasm and water down his commitment.

2. *Be candid, but don't make flat assertions.* This sounds easier than it is. When we're candid, we tend to make flat-out statements ("That's never going to work."). Don't weaken your credibility by exaggeration. Be precise.
3. *Be ready to be challenged.* This salesperson will ask tough questions, request proof, and tell you things you don't want to hear. The session can be very demanding.
4. *Use the full range of probes.* You might find open-end probes and summaries especially useful, but you'll probably need every probe.
5. *Change your strategy if his behavior shifts.* He's only human. His behavior can and may move to another quadrant. Be ready.

Development Is Incremental

Don't expect startling or dramatic results from coaching. People develop incrementally; that is, change happens in small steps, each possible only because of the one that preceded it. Human development takes place this way. It's evolutionary, not revolutionary. Only when small changes accumulate is any significant change noticeable.

Because development is incremental, you must be prepared to tolerate setbacks. There are no fool-proof development techniques. No matter how carefully you plan and direct things, you're virtually certain to encounter temporary blockages, or even reversals.

Finally, patience is a must. It's unrealistic to complain, as some sales managers do ("I sent her to a seminar last week and don't see any results."). It may be months or longer before results are visible.

The seminars we conduct, based on the principles in this book, offer a good example. They are intensive. For three to four days, participants work at developing timing skills, probing skills, presentation-planning skills, and so on. Yet, in most cases, no noteworthy results are observed in the first week or even a month after the seminar. The participants return to work, and nothing much seems to happen. Why not?

For two reasons:

1. *It's well documented that it is difficult to replace habitual behaviors with skills learned in a seminar.* The habitual behaviors feel comfortable, whereas the new skills feel awkward. The habitual behaviors can be performed without even thinking. The new skills can be performed only with a certain amount of effort. Not surprisingly, then, many people return to work and find themselves using a mixture of "easy" old behaviors and "hard" new ones.
2. *The skills they learned in the seminar have not yet been perfected.* A seminar can only teach skills in a basic way. Back on the job, the skills must be sharpened and improved. This is especially true of human relationship skills. They can only take hold through steady practice and application. Even if a brash and arrogant salesperson decided to use immediately the Q4 skills learned at a seminar, how realistic is it to assume her customers will respond to this about-face right away?

A Final Thought

At best, coaching is hard to do, no matter what the salesperson's behavior. It usually requires you to question a person's past performance or way of doing things. It often involves criticism, which is seldom enjoyable to hear, even when it is handled in a Q4 manner. And it requires change, which is rarely easy.

That's why self-discovery is so important. If you can get the salesperson to call his own performance into question, to analyze it, and to realize for himself that change is required, you stand a much better chance of conducting effective coaching. However, you can't guide anyone to self-discovery without excellent probing skills.

If we have made one point over and over in this book, it's that probing is not a fringe activity. It's at the very heart of successful sales management and successful selling. It deserves all the practice you can give it.

What's Next?

Although all the major concepts in this book may seem reasonable and logical, you might still be wondering if they can really have a positive result and make a difference in sales and managing salespeople. We conclude the book by answering those questions.

CHAPTER 15

What's in it for You?

With all that you now know about Q4 behavior and our own belief that it will benefit you both as a salesperson and a sales manager, you may still wonder whether Q4 skills really work. Can they help you get a bigger payoff from your efforts?

The answer is yes, as we'll demonstrate in this chapter. More than that, we'll explain how you can make Q4 skills part of your everyday routine. After all, putting the ideas of this book to use, not merely reading about them, is what is important.

What's the Evidence?

A large number of major corporations use our sales training programs to teach their salespeople the Q4 skills and concepts in this book. Because many of these organizations are eager to benefit from participating in our seminars, they maintain close follow-up activities to track the results of learning Q4 sales training techniques. Figure 31 (page 226) is a composite of the findings of a number of these companies.

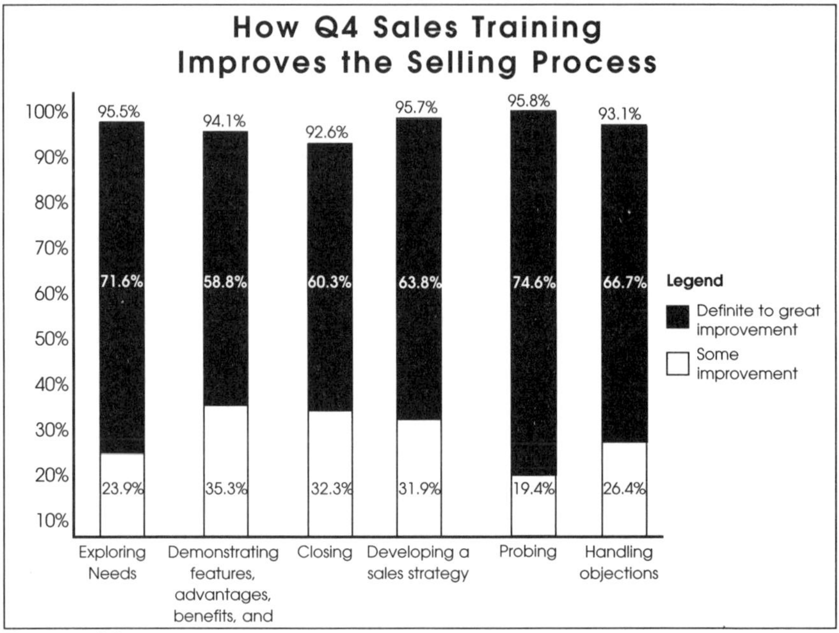

Figure 31

The figure makes two things clear:

1. *Those who go through a Q4 sales seminar find the skills useful, provided they are used.* If applied on the job, the skills taught in this book can improve sales performance.
2. *Although all the skills are useful, probing skills are the most useful.* That's probably because they're components of every other skill. If you don't know how to probe, you cannot perform Q4 exploring of needs, Q4 demonstrating of benefits, Q4 closing, or Q4 anything else. Probing skills are fundamental.

Figure 32 (page 227) provides additional evidence for the usefulness of Q4 sales behavior. The "real-life case" refers to this: In our seminar, each salesperson selects an actual prospect or customer, a real target account, that meets two criteria — the prospect or customer must represent good sales potential, and the potential must so far have proven impossible to convert into a sale. It's someone the salesperson is supposed to sell but can't.

Working with his seminar team, the salesperson plans a detailed Q4 strategy for making this "impossible" sale. During the seminar, he practices the strategy and fine-tunes it. After the seminar, he uses the strategy in the field with the real prospect or customer. Figure 32 shows how many of these strategies have produced closed sales in four major, but varied, companies.

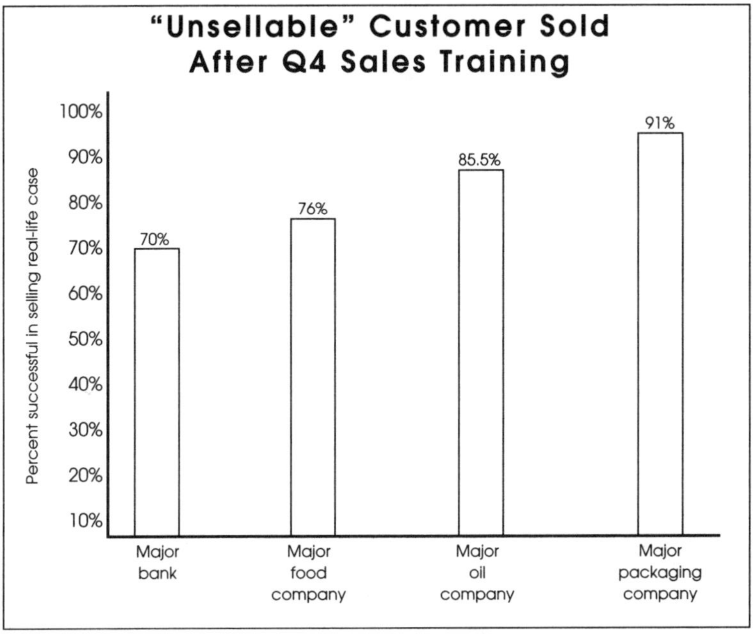

Figure 32

The figure is a good illustration of two points:

1. *A remarkable number of "unsellable" prospects, those whom experience shows cannot be closed, are actually reachable and can be closed when Q4 skills are used.* Very frequently, the salesperson in effect is saying, "I've called on that prospect using a Q1, Q2, or Q3 approach and found that it doesn't work." When the same salesperson tries again using a Q4 approach, the results are very often reversed.
2. *The format used for planning the Q4 sales strategy can be used repeatedly.* It's not a one-shot device. It can be applied again and again.

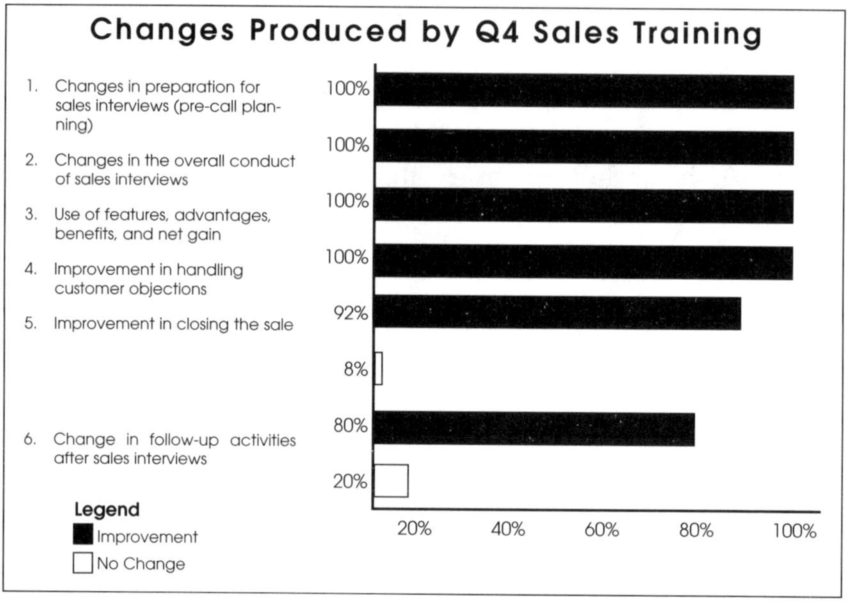

Figure 33

Figure 33 offers still further evidence of the value of Q4 skills. It details the experience of a major oil company that has used Q4 training for many years. As the first four items show, all the salespeople who have gone through the program have used Q4 sales skills to change the way they prepare for calls, conduct calls, present benefits, and handle objections. Have these changes improved results? In 92 percent of the cases (Item 5), Q4 skills have helped close sales.

From all of this evidence and much more that is available, it's clear that Q4 skills do work and will help you get a bigger payoff from your selling efforts. But you have to put them to use. How can you do it? By applying systematic self-development. The rest of the chapter will explain this.

Four Ways of Self-Development

By definition, to develop yourself means to make improvements in yourself, whether dramatic or subtle. Most change in your behavior involves the following:

1. *Bridging the self-perception gap.* We can best explain the self-perception gap by urging you to re-take the questionnaire on your own sales behavior, which appeared in Chapter 1. If you do, you are apt to discover that your present behavior isn't what you want it to be, that you usually display more Q1, Q2, or Q3 behavior and less Q4 behavior than you'd like. That's a self-perception gap — a realization that there's a distance between where you are now and where you'd like to be. The simple diagram shown in Figure 34 should help you visualize what we're talking about.

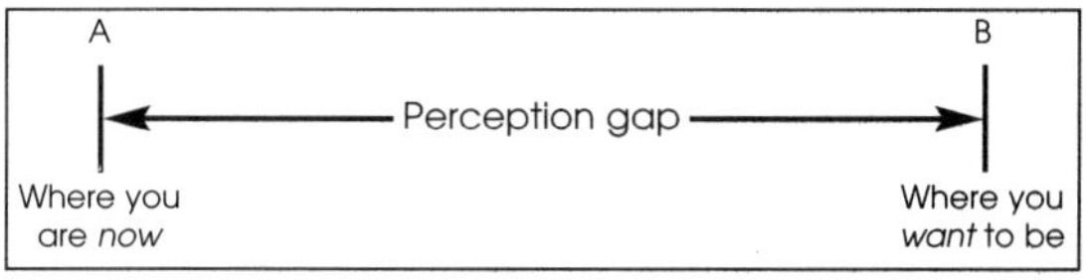

Figure 34

Point A is your present behavioral position, the way you typically interact now with customers or salespeople. It may be largely Q1, Q2, or Q3, or some combination of them. Point B is your ideal behavioral position, the way you'd like to interact. We'll assume that B consists entirely, or at least largely, of desirable Q4 behavior.

Experiencing a self-perception gap is actually a good thing. Most self-development begins with a dissatisfaction with the gulf between our actual behavior and our ideal behavior. This isn't surprising. As we've discussed, we all are motivated to do things when we feel they will fill a need and make us better off.

If you perceive yourself at point A, but would like to be at point B, there's only one way to close the gap — by mastering Q4 skills. They are the bridge that will close the gap.

To start the process of self-development, then, ask yourself whether you would get a bigger payoff for your efforts if you exerted more Q4 skills more often. If the answer is yes, you have all the reason you need to master Q4 skills.

2. *Practice.* This is essential. Any bridge between your behavior and Q4 behavior will be tenuous unless you consistently practice Q4

behavior. All behavior, whether playing the piano, selling, or managing salespeople, must be practiced over and over to become genuinely effective. There are no short cuts.

3. *Modeling.* The power of example is important in changing behavior. If you want to make your behavior more Q4, single out people in your company who display Q4 behavior. Then, watch them in action. Note the way they interact with others or with you in meetings, discussions, under stress, and so on. You don't want to copy their behavior, but emulate it. Use it as a basic pattern for your own.
4. *Feedback.* Seek out feedback about your behavior from people in your company, friends, and relatives who display Q4 behavior and whose opinion you respect. Explain that you've embarked on a program of self-development and would like their help. If what they tell you doesn't seem fully candid, try out your probing skills in an effort to increase their candor. The truth may sting a little, but there's no better way to find out what you're doing that you should do differently.

The Need for Q4 Goals

If mastering Q4 skills is the way to close your self-perception gap, you need to develop Q4 goals. However, "I want to be a better salesperson" is not a Q4 goal. Neither is "I want to get ahead in my company." These are wishes, hopes, or aspirations; but they are not Q4 goals because they don't require optimal effort. They're not specific, and they're not comprehensive. Q4 goals must be operational. They must lead to specific actions.

This technique should prove useful in closing the self-perception gap:

1. *List a couple of specific business events facing you in the coming week.* If you're a salesperson, pick sales calls. If you're a sales manager, pick coaching sessions.
2. *Spell out on paper your goals in the events you've selected.* Write out the goals in Q4 terms.

3. *Develop a plan of action for achieving each goal.* Make certain the plan incorporates the use of Q4 skills.
4. *Repeat the process the next week.* This time, pick three or four events. Keep expanding your use of Q4 skills each week until they become second nature. Figure 35 shows a couple examples.

Plan of Action

Event	Goal	Plan-of-Action
(For salesperson) August 4: Sales call on Hal Casper of Federal Plastics	Persuade Casper to replace his current extrusion equipment with our model 270G; get signed agreement to have new equipment delivered and in operation by December 15.	1. Plan and practice presentation evening of August 3. 2. Review plan shortly before call. 3. Follow the Structured Sales Call Format during the call. Be especially sure to probe carefully during step 2; Casper is usually tight-lipped about his needs. 4. Rely heavily on the Q4 strategy for Q2 behavior (unless Casper's behavior changes during course of call).
(For sales manager) August 6: Performance review for Delores Holt	Find out why Delores' sales have slumped 20% in the last 3 months. Work out plan-of-action to bring sales up to former level.	1. Review chapter on probing in *Dimensional Selling* book. 2. Write out examples of probes that would be especially helpful in finding out what's happened to Delores' sales. Remember her receptivity will probably be low. 3. Practice these probes on tape recorder the evening before the meeting. 4. Follow the sales call format during the meeting. Use the Q4 strategy for Q1 behavior.

Figure 35

Set your own Q4 goals, work out your own action plans, and follow through. There's no other way to get from where you are today to where you want to be.

The Importance of Doing

This brings us to our final point. It takes more than reading to develop Q4 skills. Knowledge gained from reading isn't know-how. Know-how is the ability to put knowledge to work to produce results. And know-how comes from doing what you've read about, applying knowledge again and again until you have the people skills we have been discussing.

The strongest claim we can make for this book, then, is that it's a start. If you set it aside and forget it, it will make no difference at all in the results you get. If you keep it near at hand and apply its principles, we confidently predict you'll develop into a more productive salesperson or sales manager. If you read it and follow it up by participating in one of our sales or sales management training seminars, we confidently predict you'll become even more productive because you will be systematically practicing Q4 skills and getting feedback.

How much more productive you will become by practicing these skills will depend on your present skills, your diligence, the support from your company, and other circumstances. Nevertheless, one thing is for certain: If you practice what you read about, you will become more productive.

It's up to you!

APPENDIX

Does the Dimensional Model Fit the Facts?

In reading this book, you may have wondered if the Dimensional Model actually fits the facts of human interaction as verified by behavioral science. The answer is yes. We'll explain how the model and the research fit together.

Every training-and-development specialist has been exposed to various models of human behavior. All the most widely used and respected ones resemble one another to a striking degree. However, no model has been subjected to as much empirical research as the model on which all Dimensional Training® is based.

This pioneering "interpersonal classification system" was developed in the late 1940s by psychologists Coffey, Freedman, Leary, and Ossorio. To see how valid this system was and develop it further, in the 1950s, the Kaiser Foundation and the U. S. Public Health Service began to sponsor a series of research projects. The final results were collated and published in 1957.

Since then, a number of other studies have amplified and tested the validity of the Kaiser research. They demonstrate that the Dimensional Model is a valid classification of interpersonal behavior and is a dependable tool for understanding that behavior.

To explain how that validation came about, we go back to the beginning.

The Early Models

In its simplest form, the interpersonal classification system developed by Coffey and his associates looked like this:

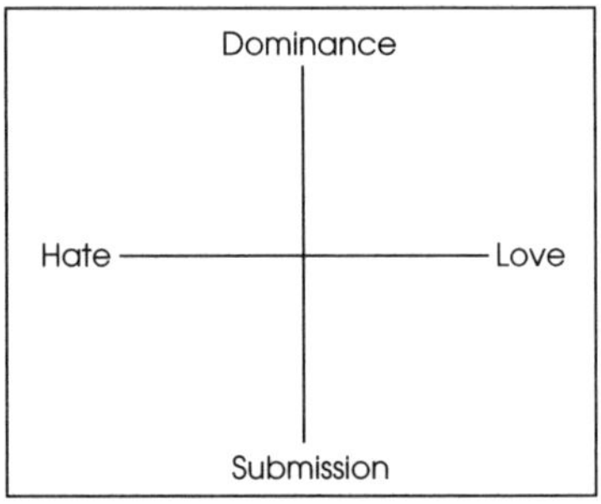

The 1957 Kaiser version of this model, based on years of additional research, was more complex. It looked like this:

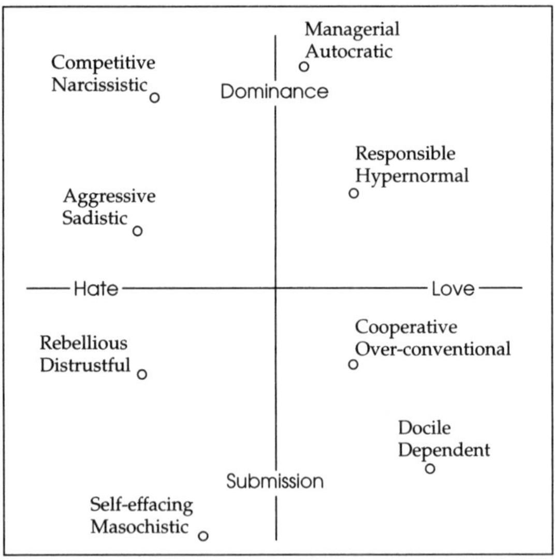

Anyone familiar with any Dimensional Training® program will quickly recognize the strong resemblance between these two models and our Dimensional Model. That is because the Kaiser research was published at the time when our consulting firm, Psychological Associates, was developing the first Dimensional

Training® program, Dimensional Sales Training. We already knew of the Coffey model and were impressed by it. When the Kaiser research appeared, it confirmed our belief that, with suitable modifications, this model could be extremely useful in describing business interactions. The modifications were necessary for two reasons:

1. *The language of neither model, the Coffey nor the Kaiser version, was entirely appropriate for business interactions.* "Hate" and "love" were obviously too strong and didn't really describe what is involved in most business transactions.
2. *The later model was too unwieldy for business use.* Eight behaviors presented no problems for clinicians and other specialists in human behavior (for whom the Kaiser research was intended), but business people needed a model that could be more readily mastered and used.

The Dimensional Model

The original Dimensional Model, then, was an adaptation of the Coffey model applied to the world of work. Moreover, it was a model based on the extensive research funded by the Kaiser Foundation. So, we knew when we developed it that the Dimensional Model had worthy ancestors. Our model in its most generalized form looks like this:

Dominance

	Q1 Behavior	**Q4 Behavior**	
	• Cocky, brash, pushy • Overcontrols • Tries to dominate others and monopolize conversations • Motivates by threat or coercion	• Strong, self-assured, dynamic • Gets other person involved • Reaches decisions through candid give-and-take • Motivates by understanding and commitment	
Hostility			Warmth
	Q2 Behavior	**Q3 Behavior**	
	• Withdrawn, indecisive, diffident • Gives in easily • Tries to avoid close interpersonal situations • Makes no effort to motivate	• Friendly, easygoing, perpetually optimistic • Doesn't argue • Seeks out close, relaxed interpersonal situations • Motivates by affection and loyalty	

Submission

Since 1958, we've adapted this model, with its now familiar quadrants or "Qs," to a variety of business behaviors. But many users of the model may have been bothered by several doubts: Can interactional behavior really be explained by only two dimensions? If so, are the two dimensions used in our model the right ones for rendering this explanation?

A series of independent studies has shown the answer to both questions to be yes. A description of a prominent independent study follows.

The Truckenmiller-Schaie Study

A report published in 1979 in the *Journal of Consulting and Clinical Psychology* on research done by Truckenmiller of Wilkes College and Schaie of the University of Southern California comes to this conclusion:

> "Our results principally confirm the general validity [of the 1957 model] with respect to the number and nature of dimensions found to subsume interpersonal behavior ratings."

The purpose of the Truckenmiller-Schaie study was to test the validity of the model that came out of the Kaiser research. Because the original report is very technical and statistical, we summarize their findings and the conclusions they reached in very general terms:

- The study involved 160 subjects from West Virginia University. They were separated into 14 groups. Each person did a self-rating and rated five other subjects on how closely they measured up to one or another of the behaviors on the model.
- To do the ratings, the subjects responded to selected items on a testing instrument called the Interpersonal Check List (ICL) and to the pictures on a group of cards known as the Thematic Apperception Test (TAT).
- In responding to the ICL items, each subject was asked to endorse or not endorse each item, depending on whether it described the person being rated.

- In responding to the TAT cards, each subject was asked, among other questions: "What is going on in the picture? How do the people feel about each other? How does the story end?"
- The subjects thus produced three different kinds of information: 1) ratings of other people's observed behavior; 2) ratings of their own behavior; and 3) imaginary analyses of interpersonal situations.

These three sources of information were then analyzed and correlated with the model. Here are the results:

1. *The ratings of other people's observed behavior and ratings of the subject's own behavior lend support to the model.*
2. *The imaginary analyses of interpersonal situations lend somewhat more modest support to the model.* These findings are hardly surprising. Ever since the first Dimensional Training® seminar, Dimensional trainers have been advising participants in analyzing behavior to focus only on observed behavior — what they've actually seen and heard — and to ignore "fantasy production" — what people imagine about behavior.

   Fantasy production is often an indulgence in wishful thinking. In the imagination, weak Walter Mittys easily become heroic earth-shakers. If a model purports to describe real behavior in the real world, as the Kaiser model does, then it's reasonable to assume that the model will receive its strongest corroboration from ratings of overt behavior.
3. *Behavior can be explained in terms of two major dimensions.*
4. *The two dimensions identified by the model (dominance-submission and love-hate) thoroughly correspond to the findings of the study.*

Significantly, Truckenmiller and Schaie don't claim that their findings stand alone. As they put it, "Our results seem consistent with a body of literature analyzing the structure of interpersonal behavior ratings." They then list a number of studies, the results of which generally coincide with their study results.

This study lends strong support to the claims that the Kaiser and Coffey models, and by extension the Dimensional Model, stand up to the real world.

Bibliography

Alessandra, Tony, Phil Wexler, and Rick Barrera. *Non-Manipulative Selling.* New York: Prentice Hall Press, 1987.

Argyris, C. *Personality and Organization.* New York: Harper & Row, 1957.

Aubuchon, Norbert. *The Anatomy of Persuasion.* New York: AMACOM, 1997.

Bachrach, Bill. "Values-Based Selling: What it Really Takes to Influence Human Behavior." *Insurance Sales,* April, 1994; 137: 63-66.

Barsky, Jonathan D. and Jonathan Barsky. *Finding Profit in Customer Satisfaction: Translating Best Practices into Bottom-Line Results.* New York: Contemporary Books, 1998.

Barsky, Jonathan D. and Jonathan Barsky. *World-Class Customer Satisfaction.* Chicago: Richard Irwin, 1994.

Bennis, W. *Changing Organizations.* New York: McGraw-Hill, 1966.

Blake, R. and Jane Mouton. *The Managerial Grid.* Houston, Texas: Gulf Publishing, 1964.

Bogdanof, Ellyn Setnor. "The Virtues of Value-Added Selling." *American Agent & Broker,* January, 1997; 69: 16-18.

Bolton, Robert. *People Skills.* New York: Simon & Schuster, 1979.

Brian, Jeffrey. "Handling the Dreaded Price Objection." *Canadian Manager,* Spring, 1997; 22: 26-27.

Bruce, Gregory and Jonathan Shermer. "Strategic Partners, Alliances Used to Find Ways to Customer Costs." *Oil & Gas Journal,* November 8, 1993; 91: 71-76.

Buzzotta, V.R., R.E. Lefton, and Manuel Sherberg. *Effective Selling Through Psychology.* St. Louis: Psychological Associates, Inc., 1982.

Buzzotta, V.R., R.E. Lefton, Alan Cheney, and Ann Beatty. *Making Common Sense Common Practice: A Leader' Guide to Using What You Already Know.* San Francisco: New Leaders Press, 1996.

Chitwood, Roy. *World Class Selling.* Minneapolis: Best Sellers Publishing, 1996.

Cialdini, Robert B. *Influence: The Psychology of Modern Persuasion.* New York: William Morrow and Company, Inc., 1984.

Collins, Michael. "Breaking into the Big Leagues." *American Demographics* (Marketing Tools Supplement), January/February, 1996; pp. 24-29.

Connellan, T. *How to Improve Human Performance.* New York: Harper & Row, 1978.

Cooper, Martha C. and John T. Gardner. "Building Good Business Relationships — More Than Just Partnering or Strategic Alliances?" *International Journal of Physical Distribution & Logistic Management,* 1993; 23: 14-26.

Corcoran, Kevin J., Laura K. Petersen, Daniel B. Baitch, and Mark F. Barrett. *High Performance Sales Organizations: Achieving Competitive Advantage in the Global Marketplace.* Chicago: Richard Irwin Professional Publishing, 1995.

Covey, Stephen R. *The Seven Habits of Highly Effective People.* New York: Fireside, 1990.

Davis, Kevin and Kenneth H. Blanchard. *Getting into Your Customer's Head: The Eight Roles of Customer-Focused Selling.* New York: Times Books, 1996.

Dudley, George W. and Shannon L. Goodson. *The Psychology of Sales Call Reluctance: Earning What You're Worth.* Washington D. C.: Behavioral Science Research, 1999.

Dudley, George W., Shannon L. Goodson, and David A. Weissenburger. "Overcoming Fear in Salespeople." *Training & Development,* December, 1993; 47: 34-38.

Fisher, Roger and Scott Brown. *Getting Together: Building Relationships As We Negotiate.* New York: Penguin Books, 1988.

Fisher, Roger and William Ury. *Getting to Yes: Negotiating Agreement Without Giving In.* New York: Penguin Books, 1981.

Geraghty, Barbara, Michael Larsen, and Fred Hills. *Visionary Selling: How to Get to Top Executives and How to Sell Them When You're There.* New York: Simon & Schuster, 1998.

Glass, Lillian. *He Says She Says: Closing the Communication Gap Between the Sexes.* New York: Perigee Publishing, 1995.

Goff, Brent G., Danny N. Bellenger, and Carrie Stojack. "Cues to Consumer Susceptibility to Salesperson Influence: Implications for

Adaptive Retail Selling." *Journal of Personal Selling & Sales Management*, Spring, 1994; 14: 25-39.

Good, Bill. *Prospecting Your Way to Sales Success: How to Find New Business by Phone, Fax, Internet, and Other New Media.* New York: Scribner, 1997.

Graham, John R. "Avoid the Sales Killers and Watch Your Sales Climb."*American Salesman*, June, 1996; 41: 8-11.

Greco, Susan. "The Art of Selling." *Inc.*, June, 1993; 15: 72-80.

Haitt, John T. "Empowering the Global Sales Force." *International Business*, September, 1994; 7: 16-20.

Hanan, Mack. *Consultative Selling.* New York: AMACON, 1995.

Heiman, Stephen E., Diane Sanchez, Tad Tuleja, Robert B. Miller, and John Philip Coghlan. *The New Conceptual Selling.* New York: Warner Books, 1999.

Herzberg, F. B., B. Mausner, and B. Snydeman. *The Motivation to Work.* New York: John Wiley, 1959.

Hogan, Kevin. *The Psychology of Persuasion.* New York: Pelican Publishing Co., 1996.

Holden, Jim. *Power Base Selling.* New York: John Wiley & Sons, Inc., 1990.

Jolles, Robert L. and Rob Jolles. *Customer Centered Selling: Eight Steps to Success from the World's Best Sales Force.* New York: Simon & Schuster, 1998.

Jolson, Marvin A. "Broadening the Scope of Relationship Selling." *Journal of Personal Selling & Sales Management*, August, 1997; pp. 39-42.

Jolson, Marvin A. "Prospecting by Telephone Prenotification: An Application of the Foot-in-the-Door Technique." *Journal of Personal Selling & Sales Management*, Fall, 1997; 17: 75-88.

Jones, Mike. "Value Added Selling." *American Agent & Broker*, December, 1994; 66: 14-15.

Jones, Thomas O. and W. Earl Sasser Jr. "Why Satisfied Customers Defect." *Harvard Business Review*, November/December, 1995; pp. 88-99.

Kagan, Norman. *Interpersonal Process Recall: A Method of Influencing Human Interaction.* Ann Arbor: Michigan State University Press, 1975.

Karrass, Chester. *Give and Take: The Complete Guide to Negotiating Strategies and Tactics.* New York: Harper Business, 1993.

Koch, Richard. "Tips on Handling the Price Objection." *Sales & Marketing Training*, August, 1988; pp. 9-11.

Kouzes, James M. and Barry Z. Posner. *Credibility.* San Francisco: Jossey-Bass Publishers, 1993.

Kurzrock, Warren. *The Sales Strategist: 6 Breakthrough Sales Strategies to Win New Business.* Chicago: Irwin Professional Publishing, 1996.

Laborde, Genie. *Influencing With Integrity.* Palo Alto, California: Syntony Publishing, 1987.

Lefton, R.E. and V.R. Buzzotta. *Leadership Through People Skills: Dimensional Management Strategies.* St. Louis, Missouri: Psychological Associates, Inc., 2000.

Lefton, R.E., V.R. Buzzotta, Manuel Sherberg, and Dean L. Karraker. *Effective Motivation Through Performance Appraisal: Dimensional Appraisal Strategies.* Cambridge, Massachusetts: Ballinger Publishing Co., 1977.

Maslow, A. H. *Motivation and Personality.* New York: Harper & Row, 1954.

McClelland, D. C., J. W. Atkinson, R. A. Clark, and E. L. Lowell. *The Achievement Motive.* New York: Appleton-Century Crofts, 1953.

McGregor, D. *The Human Side of Enterprise.* New York: McGraw-Hill, 1960.

Metcalf, Tom. "Value-Added Selling: Make Yourself the Expert." *Life Association News,* December, 1996; 91: 14-17.

Miller, Robert B., Stephen E. Heiman, and Tad Tuleja. *Conceptual Selling.* Berkeley, California: Miller-Heiman, Inc., 1987.

Miller, Robert B., Stephen E. Heiman, and Tad Tuleja. *Strategic Selling.* New York: William Morrow and Company, Inc., 1985.

Mills, Harry A. *Artful Persuasion.* New York: AMACOM, 2000.

Monkerud, Don. "Time for Team Selling." *Editor & Publisher,* October 12, 1996; 129: 32A-34A.

Mullin, Rick. "Taking Customer Relations to the Next Level." *Journal of Business Strategy,* January/February, 1997; 18: 22-26.

Nichols, Ralph G. and Leonard Steven. *Are You Listening?* New York: McGraw-Hill, 1957.

Parinello, Anthony and Denis Waitley. *Selling to VITO (The Very Important Top Officer),* 2nd. ed. Holbrook, Massachusetts: Adams Media Corporation, 1999.

Pavone, Leo. "Go Beyond Satisfaction or Lose Your Customers." *Best's Review,* January, 1995; 95: 70-72.

Peoples, David A. *Selling to the Top: David Peoples' Executive Selling Skills.* New York: John Wiley & Sons, 1993.

Petrone, Joe. *Building the High-Performance Sales Force.* New York: Productivity Management Press, 1994.

Rackham, Neil. *SPIN Selling.* New York: McGraw-Hill, Inc., 1988.

Rackham, Neil and John R. Devincentis. *Rethinking the Sales Force: Redefining Selling to Create and Capture Customer Value.* New York: McGraw-Hill, Inc., 1999.

Rackham, Neil, Lawrence Friedman, and Richard Ruff. *Getting Partnering Right: How Marketing Leaders Are Creating Long-Term Competitive*

Advantage. New York: McGraw-Hill, Inc., 1996.

Robert, Lee R. "Men Selling to Women and Women Selling to Women." *Insurance Sales,* November, 1994; 137: 8-12.

Rochford, Linda and Thomas R. Wotruba. "New Product Development Under Changing Economic Conditions: The Role of the Salesforce." *Journal of Business & Industrial Marketing,* 1993; 8: 4-12.

Rogers, Carl R. *On Becoming a Person.* New York: Houghton Mifflin Co., 1961.

Sadovsky, Marvin C. and Jon Caswell. *Selling the Way Your Customer Buys: Understand Your Prospects Unspoken Needs and Close Every Sale.* New York: AMACOM, 1996.

Scott, Michael P. "Relationship Selling." *Executive Excellence,* January, 1995; 12: 18.

Sewell, Carl and Paul B. Brown. *Customer for Life: How to Turn That One-Time Buyer into a Lifetime Customer.* New York: Doubleday, 1990.

Sharma, Arun and Rajnandini Pillai. "Customers' Decision-Making Styles and Their Preference for Sales Strategies: Conceptual Examination and an Empirical Study." *Journal of Personal Selling & Sales Management,* Winter, 1996; 16: 21-33.

Smith, Homer B. *Selling Through Negotiation.* Chevy Chase, Maryland: Marketing Education Associates, 1988.

Stevens, Nancy J. and Bob Adams. *Customer-Focused Selling.* New York: Adams Media Corporation, 1997.

Stowell, Daniel M. *Sales Marketing & Continuous Improvement: Six Best Practices to Achieve Revenue Growth and Increase Customer Loyalty.* San Francisco: Jossey-Bass, 1997.

Teich, Irwin. "Holding on to Customers: The Bottom-line Benefits of Relationship Building." *Bank Marketing,* February, 1997; 29: 12-13.

Tingley, Judith C. *Genderflex: Men & Women Speaking Each Other's Language at Work.* New York: AMACON, 1994.

Trainor, Norm. *The 8 Best Practices of High Performing Sales People.* New York: John Wiley & Sons, 2000.

Tracy, Brian. *Advanced Selling Strategies.* New York: Fireside, 1996.

Ury, William. *Getting Past No: Negotiating With Difficult People.* New York: Bantam Books, 1991.

Verba, Sidney. *Small Groups and Political Behavior.* Princeton, New Jersey: Princeton University Press, 1961.

Webster, Frederick E. Jr. "Executing the New Marketing Concept." *Marketing Management,* 1994; 3: 8-16.

Werth, Jacques and Nicholas E. Ruben. *High Probability Selling: Re-Invents the Selling Process.* New York: Abba Publishing Company, 1997.

Whitmore, John. *Coaching for Performance.* London: Nicholas Brealey, 1996.
Whyte, W. H. *The Organization Man.* New York: Simon and Schuster, 1956.
Zeithaml, Valerie A., A. Parasuraman, and Leonard L. Berry. *Delivering Quality Service: Balancing Customer Perceptions and Expectations.* New York: Free Press, 1990.

INDEX